Note-A-

365 VOICE LESSONS

2009 EDITION

by Elizabeth Lavenue
with David Franklin

Table of Contents/Preface

Introduction	1
About the Author	2
Useful Information	3
Glossary	4
Improvisation	6
The Three Areas for the Singer-Actor	7
Spelling Scales and Chords	8
Scales	9
Circle of Fifths	10
Reading Rhythms	11

Introduction

Thanks for picking up the Note-A-Day Calendar for Voice! We're excited to offer this updated edition, with dates and new trivia for 2009.

The lessons inside are simple and straightforward, and each one can be completed in five minutes or less. Want to stretch a lesson further? Pressed for time? Use what's presented here as a starting point to modify or supplement as you like. And, if you don't have time for a lesson, you can at least add a new piece of music trivia to your repertoire!

In the next several pages, you'll find some terms, theory, and other useful information to help you get the most out of this calendar. Read this before starting; it should only take a few minutes.

Got something you'd like to see in next year's edition? Submit a lesson, and you'll receive a free 2010 calendar!

Thanks for singing!

About the Author

Elizabeth Lavenue is a singer, actor, dancer, and voice teacher. An Oregonian for the past 20 years, Elizabeth has studied, taught and performed both Western and Eastern music.

Elizabeth is a graduate of Lewis & Clark College, the Wesley Balk MT Institute, and a member of NATS, the National Association for Teachers of Singing. She started her career as a performer with Portland Opera's educational programs and with various musical theatre and comedy groups. As a Certified Teacher with the Northwest Institute of Voice, she blends together her experience as a voice teacher and performer with her love of facilitating people to reach beyond their limitations. Elizabeth offers a new path of vocal exploration that leads singers right to their hearts.

In addition to teaching individual voice lessons, she also teaches music and movement to preschoolers and their families in Music Together classes. Her performing duo, the Humble Divas, performs original political musical comedy.

For information about private lessons, workshops, or performances, visit www.elizabethlavenue.com, call 503-282-9668, or email elavenue@comcast.net.

Useful Information

- Some lessons require doing additional research. Part of becoming a better singer is learning where and how to look for the information you need. Be creative! Libraries, books, music stores, teachers, the Internet, other singers, friends, and videos are places to look. In many cases, we also mention useful links as part of the lesson. For more resources, visit our website: www.Note-A-Day.com.

- Essential things to have available: a pitch pipe (used for finding pitches without a keyboard) or keyboard; metronome; stereo or boom box; and a journal or notebook.

- While you don't need to be able to read music in order to do the lessons, understanding rhythms will help. See page 11 for more information.

- When choosing accompaniment for your singing, you can accompany yourself on an instrument (guitar, piano, etc.) if you want, but you'll be able to focus more on your singing if your attention is not split. You can also record yourself playing the accompaniment and sing along with it. Live accompaniment is great (with someone else on the piano), but not always easy to find. Try using accompaniment CDs that are professionally made. You'll receive excellent quality, with the consistency of style and musicality that you need when practicing.

Glossary

Arpeggio: 'broken chord'; playing each note of a chord separately, often sequentially, e.g., C, E, G for a C major chord.

Circle of Fifths: an arrangement of all 12 pitch names that shows any adjacent pair of pitch names (as you move clockwise around the circle) to be a perfect fifth (see page 10).

Eight tone scale: a scale that ascends and descends a full octave (e.g., D major: D, E, F#, G, A, B, C#, D, C#, B, A, G, F#, E, D).

Five tone scale: a scale that ascends and descends five notes (e.g., C major: C, D, E, F, G, F, E, D, C).

Larynx (pronounced LAIR-inks): the voice box, housing the vocal folds and protecting the trachea.

Glossary

Pharynx (pronounced FAIR-inks): a fibromuscular tube extending above the larynx, where most of the voice resonates.

Registration: the coordination of the low and high registers of the voice, resulting in a clear, natural sound.

Resonation: the amplification, in the pharynx, of the vibrational wave of the vocal folds.

Root/tonic: the first note when spelling a chord or scale (e.g., the root of C major is C, the root of D major is D).

Scat singing: a jazz solo of vocal nonsense syllables.

Tessitura: the part of the vocal register where the majority of the notes of a melody or a voice part lie.

Improvisation

There are improvisation lessons throughout the calendar. Improvisation is simple, but not necessarily easy. So, why "study" improvisation?

- It's playful and teaches you how to "let go."
- It increases skills: listening, dramatic, verbal, knowledge of style, of composer, of subject, and of self.
- It challenges your creativity.
- It recaptures spontaneity with a "tired" piece.
- It increases your confidence.
- It's great practice for staying in the moment.
- It can help you develop different rehearsal techniques.
- Improvisation is an end in itself.

To improvise, sing any note. Next, sing another note. You've just improvised! (Ok, so it might not make you the next "American Idol").

Improvisation takes practice, and trial and error. If you're new to improvisation, start slowly; your skill will develop as you continue to practice. For all improvisation lessons, sing for at least five minutes.

The Three Areas for the Singer-Actor

Some of the tips in the calendar explore the art of musical theater.

As singers, we often work directly towards performance-readiness, without allowing ourselves time to explore and prepare.

As you play with the ideas presented, imagine that there are three areas: Exploring, Preparing, and Performing.

Start with Exploring; when you're ready, move on to Preparing, and then finally to Performing.

- **Exploring**: play with the ideas freely, no strings attached.

- **Preparing**: take the ideas you liked from your exploration, and practice them until you feel comfortable with them as performing choices.

- **Performing**: put everything together, focusing on the details.

Spelling Scales and Chords

Here are two methods of spelling scales and chords:

1. Use a formula relative to the major scale with the same root:

    The major scale has the formula 1, 2, 3, 4, 5, 6, 7
    The minor scale has the formula 1, 2, b3, 4, 5, b6, b7
    ("b" = down one half-step, "#" = up one half-step)

Start with the major scale, then use the formula. For example, to spell a C minor scale:

C	D	E	F	G	A	B	= C Major scale (refer to Circle of Fifths on page 10)
1	2	3	4	5	6	7	= Major scale formula
1	2	b3	4	5	b6	b7	= minor scale formula
C	D	Eb	F	G	Ab	Bb	= C minor scale

2. Use a formula of half-steps and whole-steps:

    H = half-step = 1 note in the chromatic scale
    W = whole-step = 2 notes in the chromatic scale

Minor scale formula = W H W W H W W

C minor scale =	C	D	Eb	F	G	Ab	Bb	C
(formula) =	(W)	(H)	(W)	(W)	(H)	(W)	(H)	

Scales (Examples in C)

Major Scale
1 2 3 4 5 6 7
W W H W W W H
C, D, E, F, G, A, B, C

Minor Scale
1 2 b3 4 5 b6 b7
W H W W H W W
C, D, Eb, F, G, Ab, Bb

Harmonic Minor Scale
1 2 b3 4 5 b6 7
W H W W H W+H H
C, D, Eb, F, G, Ab, B

Melodic Minor Scale
1 2 b3 4 5 6 7
W H W W W W H
C, D, Eb, F, G, A, B

Diminished Scale
1 b2 b3 3 b5 5 6 b7
H W H W H W H W
C, Db, Eb, E, Gb, G, A, Bb

Whole Tone Scale
1 2 3 #4 #5 #6
W W W W W W
C, D, E, F#, G#, A#

Algerian Scale
1 2 b3 4 5 b6 b7
W H W W H W W
C, D, Eb, F, G, Ab, Bb

Byzantine Scale
1 b2 b3 4 5 b6 7
H W W W H W H
C, Db, Eb, F, G, Ab, B

Hirajoshi Scale
1 2 3 #4 5 6 b7
W W W H W H W
C, D, E, F#, G, A, Bb

Mongolian Scale
1 2 4 5 6 b7
W W+H W W H W
C, D, F, G, A, Bb

Chromatic Scale
1 b2 2 b3 3 4 b5 5 b6 6 b7 7
H H H H H H H H H H H H
C, C#/Db, D, D#/Eb, E, F, F#/Gb, G, G#/Ab, A, A#/Bb, B

Major Pentatonic Scale
1 2 3 5 6
W W W+H W W+H
C, D, E, G, A

Minor Pentatonic Scale
1 b3 4 5 b7
W+H W W W+H W
C, Eb, F, G, Bb

Ionian Mode
1 2 3 4 5 6 7
W W H W W W H
C, D, E, F, G, A, B

Dorian Mode
1 2 b3 4 5 6 b7
W H W W W H W
C, D, Eb, F, G, A, Bb

Phrygian Mode
1 b2 b3 4 5 b6 b7
H W W W H W W
C, Db, Eb, F, G, Ab, Bb

Lydian Mode
1 2 3 #4 5 6 7
W W W H W W H
C, D, E, F#, G, A, B

Mixolydian Mode
1 2 3 4 5 6 b7
W W H W W H W
C, D, E, F, G, A, Bb

Aeolian Mode
1 2 b3 4 5 b6 b7
W H W W H W W
C, D, Eb, F, G, Ab, Bb

Locrian Mode
1 b2 b3 4 b5 b6 b7
H W W H W W W
C, Db, Eb, F, Gb, Ab, Bb

Circle of Fifths

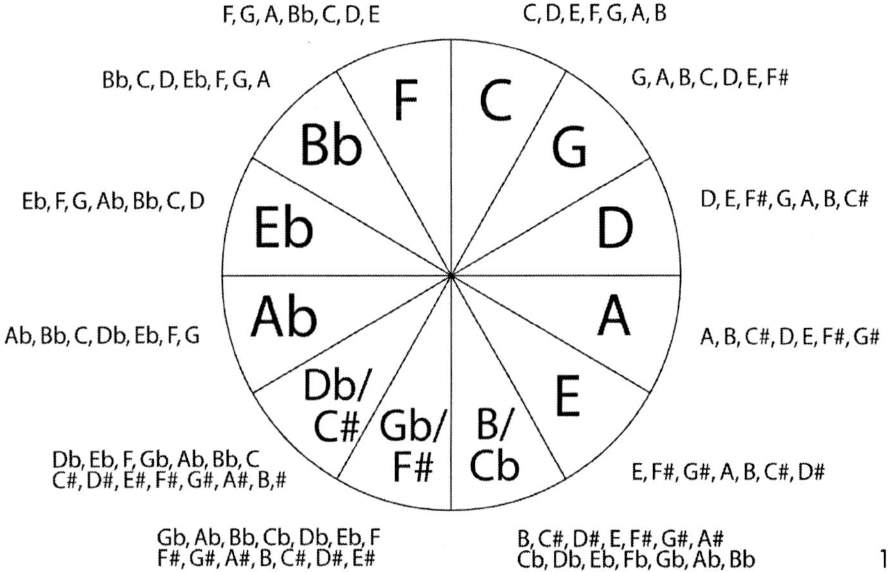

Reading Rhythms

While there are many time signatures (numeric indicators of number and length of beats), 4/4 (or C for common time) is the only one used in this calendar. To understand how this works:

Clap evenly, or turn on a metronome. Each clap or click equals one beat. In 4/4 time, four beats equal one measure.

Below are four measures, each separated by a barline. Clap and count 1-2-3-4 for each measure. While clapping, sing "la" for the note written (don't worry about the pitch) when you get to each number that's underlined. Hold the note until you get to the next one.

Whole-notes last for 4 beats = 1 per measure = 1 per every 4 clicks
Half-notes last for 2 beats = 2 per measure = 1 per every 2 clicks
Quarter-notes last for 1 beat = 4 per measure = 1 per every click
Eighth-notes last for 1/2 beat = 8 per measure = 2 per click
Sixteenth-notes last for 1/4 beat = 16 per measure = 4 per click

2009 CALENDAR

Note-A-Day Calendars

Thursday

January

1

2009

Write down your musical goals. Create one-month goals, six-month goals, one-year goals, and five-year goals. It might help to think of long-term goals first, then break those down into shorter ones.

On the first day of each month review your goals. Are you on track? Are there any adjustments you need to make in order to reach them? Are there any you want to change? Have you reached any of them?

Update your goals as necessary, and continue to review them each month (there will be a reminder on the page at the beginning of each month).

The term vocalist describes one who makes melodic and non-melodic sounds. It generally includes anyone using his or her voice as part of a musical composition, including spoken word, death grunt, and rapping.

Thursday

December

31

2009

As the year closes, reflect on all the work that you've done this year to improve as a musician and as a person. Congratulate yourself - you are doing great!

"For me, singing sad songs often has a way of healing the situation. It gets the hurt out in the open into the light, out of the darkness." - Reba McEntire

Friday

January

2

2009

If you play an instrument, accompany yourself as you sing a familiar song.

As you practice, go back and forth between practicing with the instrument and without it, noticing if your singing changes while you are playing. Work towards consistency of vocal quality.

"Music is a higher revelation than all wisdom and philosophy. Music is the electrical soil in which the spirit lives, thinks and invents." - Ludwig van Beethoven

Note-A-Day Calendars

Wednesday
December
30
2009

Find a beautiful natural area or feature that inspires you, such as a lake, stream, mountain, tree, etc. Improvise something and/or create a song that reflects how you feel about this place.

Sonny and Cher were initially known as Caesar and Cleo.

Saturday

January

3

2009

End your practice session today (and everyday) with a success. You don't need to practice a breakthrough "one more time" to see if you can do it again.

"A painter paints pictures on canvas. But musicians paint their pictures on silence." - Leopold Stokowski

Note-A-Day Calendars

Tuesday

December

29

2009

As we create vibrations through singing or chanting, the sound magnifies our intentions.

Begin today by setting an intention (it could be for yourself or others), and then sound that intention with the power of your voice.

"Do not fear mistakes. There are none." - Miles Davis

Note-A-Day Calendars

Sunday

January

4

2009

Vibrato is a naturally occurring oscillation of the vocal folds.

Sing part of a song with vibrato, then part without it. What feels most natural to you?

The ability to sing with or without vibrato will give you maximum vocal freedom, depending on the musical style.

"Music expresses feeling and thought, without language. It was below and before speech, and it is above and beyond all words." - Robert G. Ingersoll

Note-A-Day Calendars

Monday

December

28

2009

Looking at the Circle of Fifths in the preface, start with an F minor scale and name every note.

Test your memory as much as possible. Go through the Bb and Eb minor scales, making note of the ones you don't have memorized.

"Silence is the fabric upon which the notes are woven." - Lawrence Duncan

Monday

January

5

2009

Notice your posture as you move through your day. What habits have you formed?

The moment you become aware of it, pause and adjust your posture so that you are lifting through the spine, yet still grounded. Bring these new habits with you into the studio.

A lead singer is one who sings the primary vocals, as opposed to a backing singer, who accompanies the lead singer.

Note-A-Day Calendars

Sunday

December

27

2009

Using your pitch pipe (see the preface), start with F as 1, and listen carefully as you play 1 3 5 8; immediately reproduce the sounds mentally (i.e., think them). Think 1 3 5 5 8

Think 5 8. Sing it. This is a perfect fourth.

Again, play 1 3 5 8. Sing 3 5 8.

Sing 3 8. This is a minor sixth.

A soprano is a singer with a voice ranging approximately from the A below middle C to C two octaves above middle C. In four-part chorale style harmony, the soprano takes the highest part, which usually encompasses the melody.

Note-A-Day Calendars

Tuesday

January

6

2009

The day of a performance:

• Respect yourself, and set boundaries if needed
• Feel good about how you look
• Don't do anything unusual or eat anything unusual
• Don't perform in new clothes or shoes (break them in ahead of time during practice)
• Arrive early to do some visualization and relaxation techniques
• Perform pieces that you know very well

During a David Bowie concert in Glasgow, Scotland, six fans, who arrived at the venue in wheelchairs, sprang to their feet as David and his group took the stage.

Saturday

December

26

2009

Make a date to go to a sheet music store and look at different styles of music.

Some music has an accompaniment CD with and without vocals. This can be very helpful in learning new music and new styles.

Purchase one piece of music that you'd like to learn.

"Wes Montgomery played impossible things on the guitar because it was never pointed out to him that they were impossible. " - Ronnie Scott

Wednesday

January

7

2009

Who is your audience? Set some goals and intentions around where you'd like to perform, what music, and what musicians you'd like to work with. Time again for another three month check-in about your progress and overall musical goals.

Queen's "Bohemian Rhapsody," which contains the famous line, "mamma mia, mamma mia, mamma mia let me go," was knocked off the No.1 position on the UK chart by Abba's "Mamma Mia."

Note-A-Day Calendars

Friday

December

25

2009

The day of an audition or performance, be sure to:

• Wear clothes and shoes that are familiar and comfortable
• Bring copies of your music, resume, and head shot (extras may be needed)
• Run through your material earlier in the day (if needed), but don't look at it just before you go on (this might add to your nervousness)
• Trust yourself!

In 1955, singer LaVern Baker proposed an unsuccessful bid to congress to change copyright laws that would prohibit white artists from singing R & B cover tunes.

Note-A-Day Calendars

Thursday

January

8

2009

Improvise using legato (smooth and connected) and staccato (short and detached).

"All deep things are song. It seems somehow the very central essence of us, song; as if all the rest were but wrappages and hulls!" - Thomas Carlyle

Thursday
December
24
2009

Practice singing the following intervals (an interval is the distance between two notes) in the keys of D minor and A minor:

minor second (m2); ½ step; Example: D to Eb
minor third (m3); 1 ½ steps; Example: D to F

On your pitch pipe, play the higher note, then the lower note. Sing both. Memorize the sound.

The first video to premier on MTV was Buggles' "Video Killed The Radio Star" on August 1, 1981.

Note-A-Day Calendars

Friday
January
9
2009

Having trouble practicing melismas (passages of rapidly moving notes)?

Don't practice them over and over. Instead, sing them on "la" and give a slight accent to every fourth note.

Falsetto is a higher range than the head voice. Although they are anatomically produced in the same way, they are distinguished by the force at which air is pushed through the folds (falsetto relies on completely relaxed vocal folds).

Wednesday

December

23

2009

As singers, we have a three-part system with which to express ourselves: the voice, the body, and the face.

If one area isn't working well, try another: if you're blocked vocally, work with the body; if you're blocked facially, work with the voice.

Let the three parts help each other- they're partners.

The head voice bridges falsetto and chest voice, without cutting out or making any audible changes in harmonics.

Note-A-Day Calendars

Saturday

January

10

2009

Sing a chromatic scale, ascending and descending, on an "o" vowel.

Using a metronome, sing it with quarter notes, eighth notes, and sixteenth notes. Make each note as clear as possible, and make each note equal in volume and quality.

Gradually increase the tempo. This is also a great warm-up exercise.

"I think music in itself is healing. It's an explosive expression of humanity. It's something we are all touched by. No matter what culture we're from, everyone loves music." - Billy Joel

Tuesday

December

22

2009

Choose a piece of music you know well. Pull out some props: a hat, a scarf, a boa, or whatever else seems fun. Sing the song switching props throughout.

Does it change the way you express yourself? If you find one or two props that you like, just use those and sing it again. Enjoy!

A band must have a minimum of ten members before being considered a "big band."

Sunday

January

11

2009

Research the history of your favorite genre of music, such as how it was created, what other music influences it, who popularized it, how it's evolved over time, etc.

In 1996, Ringo Starr appeared in a Japanese advertisement for apple sauce, which coincidentally is what "ringo" means in Japanese.

Note-A-Day Calendars

Monday

December

21

2009

Take at least 10 minutes today and listen to three singers of contrasting styles (e.g., Frank Sinatra, Christina Aguilera, Cecilia Bartoli, etc.).

Listen with your full attention. What do you like? What might you do differently? There are no absolutes.

Bel canto is an elegant Italian vocal style emphasizing great vocal agility.

Monday

January

12

2009

Sing a piece of music for someone. Ask them what they like and don't like about the piece and how you sang it. Use their feedback to improve, remembering QTIP: Quit Taking it Personally!

Gene Simmons of Kiss has a tongue that is seven inches long, two inches longer than most men.

Sunday

December

20

2009

How often do you rest your voice during practice?

Building your voice is similar to building muscles at the gym. Work some, then rest. You need to rest at least 15 seconds between exercises to let the muscles recover.

"Modern music is as dangerous as narcotics." - Pietro Mascagni

Note-A-Day Calendars

Tuesday

January

13

2009

Singers are inspired by many different art forms, not just musical ones. Visual arts, dance, theatre, film, and performance art are just a few.

Take some time today to experience one of your favorite artistic forms. What are some of the ways this inspires you? How can this inspiration enliven your singing?

In a rondo, the first section of music recurs later, and often repeatedly, in the musical piece.

Saturday

December

19

2009

Our voice has three main areas that need to maintain balanced proportions with one another for correct functioning:

1) The Power Source: our support system, including numerous muscle systems that move the abdominal bulk up against the diaphragm.
2) The Oscillator: our vocal folds, which vibrate very rapidly as tiny puffs of air move through them.
3) The Resonator: the pharynx and mouth, where the frequencies from the vocal folds resonate and create our unique voice.

When this system is in balance, the result will be a natural sound with vibrato.

Altos originally sang from music written in the alto clef, but now use the treble clef.

Wednesday

January

14

2009

Choose a piece you know well and sing along to a metronome to help you stay in the “rhythmic pocket”.

Follow it closely. If you’re dragging behind, is it because of breathing? Late consonants? Unconscious habits?

Repeat several times, finding the “rhythmic pocket.”

“Remember, information is not knowledge; knowledge is not wisdom; wisdom is not truth; truth is not beauty; beauty is not love; love is not music; music is the best.” - Frank Zappa

Note-A-Day Calendars

Friday

December

18

2009

How grounded do you feel today?

Check in with your body, your legs, and your feet. Take a moment to focus on your feet: stretch your toes up and down, roll them from front to back and side to side, and stretch the top of your foot by curling the toes under. Then roll your ankles in both directions, stand tall and breathe down through your feet, imagining a line of energy pouring from your feet into the earth.

Singing involves a lot of energy moving upward and outward. Keeping the channel open from the top of your head to your feet will help you keep your energy grounded and renewed.

Crescendo means "increasing in loudness."

Thursday

January

15

2009

As a singer-actor, your body is your instrument. Choose clothes that are flattering, comfortable, and reflect the character you're auditioning for. This is not a costume, but a more subtle reflection of the character's style and taste, appropriate for the style of music you are singing. Sell yourself, but don't draw so much attention to your clothes that the auditioners won't even notice your voice!

Melisma occurs when several notes are sung to a single syllable.

Note-A-Day Calendars

Thursday
December
17
2009

Put on a recording of a song you are learning and dance to it.

Scan through your body and move each part of it to the music. If you feel tense anywhere, stretch, breathe deeply, and relax that area. Lose yourself in the music and quiet your mind.

Dance through the song several times, then sing it again. Notice how your singing has changed.

Ethnomusicology is the comparative study of world music, with a focus on cultural context.

Note-A-Day Calendars

Friday
January
16
2009

Review the "Three Areas" from the preface.

As you sing a song you know well, move between stillness and motion. Start with the extremes: completely still, then moving all around.

Slowly, begin moving between the two extremes, creating new blends of the two. You may arrive at choices you would like to use in performance.

"Music, once admitted to the soul, becomes a sort of spirit, and never dies."
- Edward George Bulwer-Lytton

Wednesday

December

16

2009

As you sing today, imagine that the sound is going back inside you, instead of out into the room. During moments of strong emotion, imagine that you are keeping the sound inside you, giving it to yourself, instead of giving it all away. What is this experience like for you?

Forte means "loud."

Note-A-Day Calendars

Saturday
January
17
2009

The day of an audition or performance, be sure to:

- Warm up properly, but don't oversing
- Allow extra time for preparation
- Know your destination clearly and arrive early

All of this will help you to be more relaxed.

The smallest interval used in Western music is the half-step, although other systems use the quarter-step as well as smaller intervals.

Tuesday

December

15

2009

Sing an A minor scale.

Next, sing the syllables do (1), mi (3), fa (4), sol (5), ti (7), do (8), with each syllable corresponding to the note in the scale.

Next, play the root (first) note on your pitch pipe (or other instrument). Sing that note, then sing (without playing) the entire scale, ascending and descending.

"Barbershop quartet singing is four guys tasting the holy essence of four individual mechanisms coming into complete agreement." - Meredith Willson

Note-A-Day Calendars

Sunday

January

18

2009

Record your entire practice session today. Listen to it, and notice both positive areas and places where you can improve. Also notice if certain areas could use more time than you spent on them.

Listen to your tone quality, rhythmic accuracy, and artistic interpretation.

Important Baroque composers include Johann Sebastian Bach, George Frederic Handel, Johann Pachelbel, and Antonio Vivaldi.

Monday

December

14

2009

Seek out some musical support in your community. Schedule a time to get together with one or more friends to make music.

This isn't about performing, or even practicing. Just enjoy making music together in a fun, relaxed way.

"In music, the passions enjoy themselves." - Nietzsche

Note-A-Day Calendars

Monday

January

19

2009

Recall your past performances, or, if you've never performed, what you imagine performing would be like.

Think back to (or imagine) one of your worst performances. How did you feel? What did you sing? What were the circumstances and conditions, such as location, audience size and demographics, temperature, atmosphere, etc.?

Now remember (or imagine) one of your best performances and ask yourself the same questions. What can you learn from comparing these two experiences? Write your insights in your journal.

A motet is a sacred piece from the Middle Ages composed for several voices.

Sunday
December
13
2009

Improvise with a song you are working on. Sing it using gibberish, nonsense syllables that sound like they could make sense, but really don't!

Louis Armstrong's nickname "Satchmo" was an abbreviation of "satchelmouth," a joke on the size of his mouth.

Tuesday

January

20

2009

A creative person must be willing to problem solve.

Record yourself singing a song. As you listen to yourself, there may be a number of things you'll notice and want to work on. Try to focus on the most obvious one first. Make a list to refer back to, and gradually work through each area.

The LP (long-playing) record was invented by Paul Goldmark in 1948. The LP is not dead yet: more than 10 million LPs are sold every year.

Note-A-Day Calendars

Saturday

December

12

2009

While blindfolded, sing a song that you have memorized. What do you notice about how your body moves, your arms gesture, and your voice expresses the music? Keep what works for you and discard the rest.

A piano covers the full spectrum of all orchestra instruments, from below the lowest note of the double bassoon to above the highest note of the piccolo.

Note-A-Day Calendars

Wednesday

January

21

2009

Some recommended books:

"This is Your Brain on Music: The Science of a Human Obsession" by Daniel J. Levitin

"Basics of Singing" by Jan Schmidt

"The Structure of Singing: System and Art of Vocal Technique" by Richard Miller

"On Singing Onstage: Technique" by David Craig

A tenor is a male singer with a high voice, typically extending from the C below middle C to the C above middle C. In four-part chorale-style harmony, it is the second lowest voice, above the bass and below the soprano and alto.

Note-A-Day Calendars

Friday

December

11

2009

Notice your thoughts as you practice today. Are you evaluating your singing? Are you feeling anything as you sing? Is your mind focused on what you're singing or is it thinking about other things?

See if you can objectively notice your thoughts, withough judging them. At the end of your practice session, write down some of your thoughts, especially ones that are negative. Simply noticing and being aware of them will allow you to let them go.

"The old jazz singers or old blues singers . . . weren't worried as much about their voice sounding perfect. They would make the song kind of fit their voice."
- Lucinda Williams

Thursday
January
22
2009

Notice how your voice feels after you've practiced for 30 - 45 minutes. Is it ready for more? Is it tired?

Be careful not to oversing. We often think that a "bigger" sound is a "better" sound. Don't fall into that trap. It can lead to vocal damage.

Always maintain a balanced system (see June 4th).
Sing your sound, not someone else's sound.

Beach Boys' leader Brian Wilson once had a giant sandbox built around his piano so that he could feel the sand beneath his feet for songwriting inspiration.

Note-A-Day Calendars

Thursday

December

10

2009

As you practice a song today, sing just the vowels (a,e,i,o,and u). Notice the smoothness of your transition from one vowel to another. Make it as legato (smooth) as possible.

Sing the song again with words. Do you notice any changes?

"My idea is that there is music in the air, music all around us; the world is full of it, and you simply take as much as you require." - Edward Elgar

Note-A-Day Calendars

Friday

January

23

2009

As we create vibrations through singing or chanting, the sound magnifies our intentions.

Before you begin today, set an intention for your practice session. Write it down and post it where you can see it. Look at it as you begin each new exercise or song.

You can sing the chorus of the Beach Boys "Surfing USA" along with Chuck Berry's "Sweet Little Sixteen".

Note-A-Day Calendars

Wednesday

December

9

2009

What is it that gets in your way of practicing? There may be a long list. If so, write it all down.

Now shift how you think a “practice” should be. Ten minutes can move you forward. Do whatever it takes for you to “get over it” and get into practicing!

“He who sings scares away his woes.” - Cervantes

Note-A-Day Calendars

Saturday

January

24

2009

Improvise with a song you are working on by choosing a set style: classical, jazz, rock, country, contemporary or blues.

Loosen it up and have some fun!

"Too many pieces of music finish too long after the end." - Igor Stravinsky

Note-A-Day Calendars

Tuesday

December

8

2009

When we speak, we often shift our eye focus as we have a change of thought.

Sing a song you have memorized and notice where your eyes focus while you sing.

Sing the song again, shifting your eye focus each time you express a new thought. Make a note of this in your music.

Bellicoso means "warlike, aggressive."

Note-A-Day Calendars

Sunday

January

25

2009

Sing an F major scale.

Next, sing the syllables do (1), re (2), mi (3), fa (4), sol (5), la (6), ti (7), do (8), with each syllable corresponding to the note in the scale.

Next, play the root (first) note on your pitch pipe. Sing the second note, then play the third note. Sing the fourth, play the fifth, etc., ascending and descending.

A hocket is a rhythmic device that enlivens rhythm by putting rests in the middle of vocal lines.

Note-A-Day Calendars

Monday

December

7

2009

Review the literature that you are practicing and performing. Are you singing music that is right for your voice type and your vocal ability? It's important to choose music that is challenging, but not over your head, as that could lead to vocal strain.

Review your list and mark each song that you consider really challenging for you. Only 20% (or less) of your music should be in this category. If needed, consult a professional.

When Elvis Presley was inducted into the U.S. Army, the U.S. government lost an estimated $500,000 in taxes for each year that Private Presley served.

Monday

January

26

2009

If you speak languages other than English, find a song(s) to learn in these languages (your local library is a good place to start).

If you want to learn a new language, check into class offerings (at local colleges) or private coaching sessions.

An oratorio is a long, semi-dramatic piece on a religious subject.

Sunday

December

6

2009

Finding the optimum pitch for your speaking voice is essential in developing your singing voice, since a speaking voice that is too low or raspy can lead to vocal strain.

Find a paragraph to read from a book (on any topic) and read it as FAST as you can. Try not to stop at all.

The natural pitch that your voice finds is your optimum speaking pitch. If it's higher than your normal pitch, try to gradually adjust to this new pitch during the day by doing this exercise again. Do this every day, until you feel you've adjusted to this new pitch center.

The melody for "Twinkle, Twinkle Little Star" was originally written by Bouin, and appeared in 1761. Mozart wrote 12 variations for it on the piano.

Note-A-Day Calendars

Tuesday

January

27

2009

It's easy to get overly analytical about our own voice, especially when we are striving for the One and Only Perfect Sound. This spells OOPS!

As you practice a song today, let yourself make sounds that you consider "wrong" or "ugly", feel free to make mistakes, or sing in silly voices. You never know when one of these sounds will be UBU (ugly but useful).

"Music is the mediator between the spiritual and the sensual life." - Ludwig van Beethoven

Note-A-Day Calendars

Saturday

December

5

2009

Improvise (scat) and play with sliding from your upper voice to your lower voice, and then from your lower voice to your upper voice. Explore the lows, explore the highs, and just slide through the middle.

The words "stanza" and "verse" can be used interchangeably.

Note-A-Day Calendars

Wednesday
January
28
2009

Look up and memorize definitions and/or notations for the following terms (www.8notes.com/glossary is a good resource) : duet, finale, fugue, largo, and marcato.

"Music cleanses the understanding, inspires it, and lifts it into a realm which it would not reach if it were left to itself." - Henry Ward Beecher

Friday
December
4
2009

Singing involves strengthening certain muscles, and releasing others.

Give yourself a massage to relax and loosen up your muscles. Start with your shoulders and use as much pressure as feels good to you. If there are any tense areas, focus on them longer. (If possible, ask someone else to massage you, or get a professional massage.)

A concert promoter in Hawaii sold one thousand tickets to a Spice Girls concert that was never scheduled. When the man was arrested, he told police that he needed the money for a nose job and a sex change.

Thursday

January

29

2009

Experiment with color while you sing today. Find some paper and colored pens, pastels, or paint.

At random times while you practice, stop and doodle with colors. Encourage your "judgmental" voice to take a rest, and let your playful inner artist come out to explore. Do certain sounds evoke feelings in a way that you can also express through color?

Madonna has the letters "MP" (standing for "Madonna's Property") and Marilyn Monroe's face tattooed on her bottom.

Note-A-Day Calendars

Thursday

December

3

2009

"Vocal glides" are especially helpful when your voice is really stiff (from illness, over-singing, etc.).

Focus on the transition across the middle of the voice, not on volume or tone. Make the transition as gentle as possible. Do this throughout the day.

Chanson is the French word for "song."

Friday

January

30

2009

As you practice a song today, focus on the consonants. Notice which are easy, and which are more challenging. Be sure to sing the consonant before the beat, and the vowel on the beat (no matter what style of music you're singing).

"Truly to sing, that is a different breath." - Rainer Maria Rilke

Note-A-Day Calendars

Wednesday

December

2

2009

Create some simple flash cards that list different emotions on each one, such as: silly, scared, joyful, angry, forgiving, etc.

Sing a song you know well. Pick up a new flash card every 10-15 seconds and express the emotion listed.

Continue to work with this, keeping the emotions you like, discarding the rest.

"Music is what feelings sound like." - Anonymous

Saturday

January

31

2009

Using a metronome, practice singing a minor scale in the following rhythms, ascending and descending: whole-, half-, quarter-, eighth-, and sixteenth-notes.

The whole-tone scale is comprised of only six notes of the octave. It consists of whole-steps between each of the tones.

Tuesday

December

1

2009

Some recommended books and journals:

"Pro Secrets of Heavy Rock Singing" by Bill Martin

"Singing Jazz: The Singers and Their Style"s by Bruce Crowther and Mike Pinfold

"Rise up Singing: the Group Singing Songbook" by Peter Blood

"The Journal of Singing: the Official Journal of the National Association of Teachers of Singing, Inc."

Review your musical goals today.

Sunday

February

1

2009

Sing an E minor scale using the syllables do (1), re (2), mi (3), fa (4), sol (5), la (6), ti (7), do (8), with each syllable corresponding to the note in the scale.

With your pitch pipe, play the root (first) note, then the second note. Sing both, using syllables do and re.

Play the root note, then the third note; sing both using do and mi.

Play the root note and the fourth note; sing both using do and fa.

Continue doing this for the whole scale,
ascending and descending.

Review your musical goals today.

Monday

November

30

2009

Research the following singers: Sarah Vaughn, Luciano Pavarotti, and Freddy Mercury. See what you can learn about their styles and contributions to singing.

Life is like music; it must be composed by ear, feeling, and instinct, not by rule.
– Samuel Butler, 19th century British novelist

Note-A-Day Calendars

Monday

February

2

2009

Spend 5 minutes writing about your discipline and freedom as a singer.

How disciplined are you with practicing? Can you do what you need to do technically? Artistically? How free are you to move into the unknown and step outside the box?

Having discipline will lead you to more freedom. If you notice areas where you can be more disciplined, write down some simple, concrete steps you can take to put yourself on track.

In very early manuscripts, a neuma was a sign that indicated pitch.

Sunday

November

29

2009

Make a detailed checklist of everything you need to bring to a performance or gig: song sheets, guitar (with cord), microphone (with cord), stands, water, etc. Keep this list in an obvious place where you can refer to it quickly and easily before each show.

Incidental music is written to accompany dramatic works.

Note-A-Day Calendars

Tuesday

February

3

2009

Work on your song today, as if it were a monologue. What are the different beats (sections) and what is your motivation in each of them? Read through all the lyrics as if you were auditioning with this monologue.

The instrumental concerto became a staple of the Baroque era. It found its strongest exponent in the works of the Venetian composer Antonio Vivaldi.

Note-A-Day Calendars

Saturday

November

28

2009

Spend at least five minutes writing about what you want to let go of from this year, and what you want to bring into the new year.

What are your dreams as an artist? What is your greatest vision of yourself in the next year?

A castrato is a male soprano, mezzo-soprano, or alto voice produced either by castration of the singer before puberty or who, because of an endocrinological condition, never reaches sexual maturity.

Note-A-Day Calendars

Wednesday
February
4
2009

How do you input information (visually, aurally, or kinesthetically)? How do you output information (visually, aurally, or kinesthetically)?

If you're working with a teacher, discuss this with him/her, and explore ways that your teacher can help you learn better based on how you input/output information. Visit www.chaminade.org/inspire/learnstl.htm, and/or type "learning styles" into a search engine to learn more.

Barbershop singing (a style of a cappella four-part harmonizing) originated in African-American communities in the U.S. around the turn of the last century, when barbershops were social gathering-places.

Note-A-Day Calendars

Friday

November

27

2009

A diphthong is a combination of two or more vowels together (such as “now,” which is a combination of three vowel sounds).

Look at a song you’re working on and find any diphthongs present. Decide how long you want to hold each vowel (it depends on the style). You may want to record yourself singing them in different ways and listen to find what you like.

Practice them slowly, and work up to your desired tempo.

In the Classical period, composers were interested in simplicity, balance, and emotions.

Note-A-Day Calendars

Thursday
February
5
2009

Sing the following patterns in the keys of A# and F:

1 3 2 4 3 4 2 1
1 2 1 4 2 1
3 1 2 3 4 2 1
5 3 4 2 1 7 1

Sing first using numbers, then using the names of the actual notes.

Frank Beard is only member of ZZ Top without a beard.

Note-A-Day Calendars

Thursday

November

26

2009

Spend some time outside with children today. Notice how free they are with their bodies and voices. Even little babies are uninhibited in expressing themselves.

Bring this feeling of joy and freedom with you into your practicing.

Among those who sang the chorus of The Beatles' "All You Need Is Love" were Marianne Faithfull, Graham Nash, Jane Asher, Patti Boyd, Keith Moon, and Mick Jagger.

Note-A-Day Calendars

Friday

February

6

2009

Singers can be affected by upper respiratory problems, such as allergies and colds. One of the differences between them is that allergies often have a clear sinus discharge that can come and go. Colds often have a colored sinus discharge and usually will last 7 to 10 days. For treatment of either, consider the option of consulting a medical professional. Your vocal health is important!

"The history of a people is found in its songs." - George Jellinek

Note-A-Day Calendars

Wednesday

November

25

2009

When preparing your resume, don't pack too much into it. Keep it to one page. If needed, separate your musical resume from your acting resume.

The difference between the tone poem and the romantic symphony is that the tone poem only consists of one long movement.

Saturday

February

7

2009

Think of an audition as a protective bubble: nothing in your personal life can touch you when you walk onto the stage and when you leave it, nothing from the audition can touch your personal life. This will allow you to leave it at the door and not obsess about if you'll get a callback, etc. Do your best, and let go of the rest.

Despite all of the hits that they've had, The Who have never had a number one record in the U.K. or the U.S..

Note-A-Day Calendars

Tuesday

November

24

2009

Listen to a professional recording of a song you are practicing, remembering that this sound has been produced in a studio. It's good to have a model of the sound you'd like to create, but don't expect that you will sound like this "polished" recording.

Write down five things you like about your voice.

Boy soprano (or treble in British English) is a young male singer with an unchanged voice in the soprano range. Occasionally, boys whose voices have changed can continue to sing in the soprano range for a period of time.

Note-A-Day Calendars

Sunday

February

8

2009

When choosing songs for an audition, have at least two songs that are contrasting (either in style, or an uptempo and a ballad). With both songs, clearly mark your favorite 16 bars and 32 bars. Don't do accapella songs, songs with only a lead sheet, or songs that need the accompanist to change the key. Make your music as easy to read as possible.

The song "Happy Birthday to You" is copyrighted, but so far there have been only two lawsuits related to its improper use.

Note-A-Day Calendars

Monday

November

23

2009

List your most significant vocal influences. Who are your models? What about them do you admire and appreciate? What qualities would you like to possess?

Pick one influence, and pretend to be that person while you sing. How do you feel when you imagine yourself as that person?

"Eventually you'll take the phrases and rhythm patterns you've copped and begin to put your own mark on them" - Eddie Van Halen

Monday

February

9

2009

For five minutes, chant a syllable (or a mantra, if you know one) over and over again.

Each time your mind wanders away, gently bring it back to the present moment, without judgment or analysis. Notice how your body and mind are affected by sound vibrations.

Avant-garde means "in the most advanced style."

Note-A-Day Calendars

Sunday

November

22

2009

Find a song that you are working on and have memorized. Listen to a recording of the song, and let your body move to the rhythm. Feel how your feet, legs, torso, arms, head, etc. naturally express the music. Then sing the song, allowing the movement to enhance your expression of the music.

"Play the music, not the instrument." - Anonymous

Note-A-Day Calendars

Tuesday

February

10

2009

When performing, it's important to maintain the energy and emotion of your character, even during the rests.

Take any song you're working on and think about the emotion you want to convey during each rest period. Sing the song with this new continuity.

Kenneth Edmonds was nicknamed "Babyface" by funk bassist Bootsy Collins.

Note-A-Day Calendars

Saturday
November
21
2009

Go busking! Choose a busy spot on a sidewalk, put out a bowl or basket, choose accompaniment (yourself, a friend, a CD, etc.) and start singing. See if anyone throws some money your way (hint: put some bills and coins in the basket before you start singing).

No songs from The Beatles' "Sgt. Pepper's Lonely Hearts Club Band" were released as singles.

Wednesday

February

11

2009

What does your “ideal” voice sound like? Feel like?

Vocal development takes great patience. Every three months, assess where you are and where you are going.

An accidental is a sign used to notate raising or lowering the pitch of a note.

Note-A-Day Calendars

Friday

November

20

2009

You learn a little bit more each time you audition or perform.

Start a page in your journal that is just for auditions and performances. After each one, quickly note any insights you had about how you did, and how you might do things differently next time.

Refer to this page for future insights.

A countertenor is an adult male who sings in the alto or soprano range, often through the use of falsetto. The term is used almost exclusively in the context of the classical vocal tradition.

Note-A-Day Calendars

Thursday

February

12

2009

Take a break today and just listen to one of your favorite vocal albums. Enjoy the beauty of singing.

The polyphonic singing tradition of Georgia in the former USSR was not originally intended for performance, but evolved out of life's important moments within society. Concert presentation of Georgian music began only a

Thursday

November

19

2009

All musicians listen to musical models to help them learn. The word "model" is not just referring to an artistic concept, but includes everything about that singer: their style, expression, tone quality, syllabic stress, being in the rhythmic "pocket", etc.

Each singer has many different models they can follow. Listen to one of yours, and notice the items listed above.

"There is no feeling, except the extremes of fear and grief, that does not find relief in music." - George Eliot

Note-A-Day Calendars

Friday
February
13
2009

Review the "Three Areas" from the preface.

In your practice today, experiment with moving between the music as it is written on the page (or the recording you have of it) and the spontaneity of expressing the music the way you want to. Sing the extremes: exactly as the music is written, then completely improvise.

Slowly, begin moving between the two extremes, creating new blends of the two. You may arrive at choices you would like to use in performance.

"Composers shouldn't think too much - it interferes with their plagiarism."
- Howard Dietz

Note-A-Day Calendars

Wednesday
November
18
2009

Work on only one song today, memorizing as much of it as you can. Challenge yourself to go beyond what you think you can do.

"Why waste money on psychotherapy when you can listen to (Bach's) "B Minor Mass"?" - Michael Torke

Note-A-Day Calendars

Saturday

February

14

2009

Find a recording of a song that you are working on and have memorized. Listen to the accompaniment, with eyes closed, simply being receptive.

Listen again, imagining yourself singing along. Then sing the song, noticing how your voice interacts with the accompaniment in new ways.

Led Zeppelin played "Stairway to Heaven" for the first time in Belfast on March 5, 1971. Bassist John Paul Jones said that the audience insteadwanted to hear something they knew and liked, such as "Whole Lotta Love."

Note-A-Day Calendars

Tuesday

November

17

2009

Experimenting with opposites, sing a verse or a part of a song you know well, as softly as possible. Then sing it loudly (without strain).

Now sing it moving back and forth between loud and soft. Did you discover anything new about how you can express the music?

Explore dynamic variations today.

"It occurred to me by intuition, and music was the driving force behind that intuition. My discovery was the result of musical perception." - Albert Einstein, when asked about his theory of relativity

Sunday
February
15

2009

When choosing a head shot for an audition, be sure to use one that looks like you (not air-brushed), that is alive in the eyes, and that can cover a variety of potential roles. Black and white photos are fine.

In 2000, George Michael paid £1.45m for the Steinway piano on which John Lennon wrote "Imagine."

Note-A-Day Calendars

Monday

November

16

2009

Compose a simple song of any length or style. Memorize it.

Yodeling is a technique that requires rapidly switching between at least two different registers many times in the same phrase, producing a distinct high-low-high-low sound.

Note-A-Day Calendars

Monday

February

16

2009

Be gentle with yourself as you practice. Let each new learning step be small enough that you are likely to succeed.

Learn one thing at a time; don't try to take two steps simultaneously.

Inuit throat-singing is done by women. Two women face each other and sing with lips almost touching, each using the other's mouth cavity as a resonator.

Note-A-Day Calendars

Sunday
November
15
2009

When the consonants T, D, L, or N are final consonants and the next word and/or syllable begin with a consonant, they must be followed by "uh." This is also true at the end of a phrase. Examples: eight(uh), all(uh), man(uh), and(uh).

Pick one song and notice when you need to add "uh" to make the word sound complete.

"If anyone has conducted a Beethoven performance, and then doesn't have to go to an osteopath, then there's something wrong." - Simon Rattle

Note-A-Day Calendars

Tuesday

February

17

2009

Sing one note for five minutes (or decide your own time frame before starting).

Consciously move the sound all around the pharynx. Sing with different vowels, volume, timbre (tone), rhythm, vibrato, etc.

Many operas in the Classical period were written and enjoyed mostly by wealthier people, as they were expensive to produce.

Note-A-Day Calendars

Saturday

November

14

2009

Looking at the scales on page 9, memorize the notes in the whole tone scale (all whole steps) and sing them, slowly at first, then increasing the tempo:
C, D, E, F#, G#, A#, C.

"The most perfect expression of human behavior is a string quartet." - Jeffrey Tate

Wednesday

February

18

2009

Practice writing the following symbols:
treble clef; sharp; flat; natural; double-sharp; double-flat.

Two of the greatest composers of polyphonic music were Leonin and Perotin at the Notre-Dame in Paris.

Note-A-Day Calendars

Friday
November
13
2009

Improvise using “in-out”:

Begin singing the music as written (for one phrase), then go outside the confines of the score melodically or rhythmically (for one phrase).

Continue moving “in-out” of the piece this way.
Sing one phrase “in” and one phrase “out.”

A nocturne is a composition, usually a serenade, which is meant to be played outside at night.

Thursday

February

19

2009

Singing is healing. Take a moment to reflect on how singing is healing for you. How has your life been transformed through singing? You may want to note this in your notebook or journal.

"The effects of good music are not just because it's new; on the contrary, music strikes us more the more familiar we are with it." - Johann Wolfgang Von Goethe

Note-A-Day Calendars

Thursday

November

12

2009

Just before a performance or gig, try to do your sound check on time. This gives you a necessary break between the sound check and the show, and insures that your audience won't see you earlier than you're ready to be seen.

" . . . the soul is the center and the source of all these emotions, it's the start of singing, it's inside us; the voice is the instrument, but it's the brain that gives the orders for our actions." - Jose Carreras

Note-A-Day Calendars

Friday
February
20
2009

Acoustic differences can play a large part in our perception of our voice. Practice singing in different rooms today (in your home, school, etc.).

Find a large space, an average space, and a small space. What vocal changes do you need to make to experience your sound as consistent from space to space?

Throat-singing uses the throat, voice, and breath to produce deep, breathy, rhythmic sounds with overtones. It is a traditional technique used by Tuvans, Mongolians, the Ainu of northern Japan, and Inuits.

Wednesday

November

11

2009

When you can sing something perfectly five times in a row, you have mastered it and are ready to move on. If you make a mistake, even on the fifth time, go back to the beginning and start again.

The Romantic period of music attempted to represent people, things, dramatic situations, and philosophical ideas.

Saturday

February

21

2009

Performance anxiety is a challenging part of being a singer. Next time you perform, look directly at the audience when you introduce your song. Once you're singing, look just above their heads. See if this helps calm your nerves (the audience won't notice that you're not looking at them).

"Although one can get very clever at home, progress comes a lot quicker if you step into a room with other people and start playing." - Steve Howe

Note-A-Day Calendars

Tuesday

November

10

2009

Make a date with yourself to go out and listen to a type of music that you aren't very familiar with.

Be brave and try something new! Notice your own feelings and/or judgments that arise as you listen. What can you learn from this experience?

In 1952, John Cage composed and presented "4′33″," a composition consisting of 4 minutes and 33 seconds of silence.

Sunday

February

22

2009

We often try to fight our performance nerves and wish them away.

Adrenalin is only “bad” when we label it that way. Instead, try and think of it as pure energy that will enhance your performance. Welcome it! Here comes the energy!

The harmonic chromatic scale includes all the notes in the major, harmonic minor, and melodic minor scales, plus a flatted second and raised fourth.

Monday

November

9

2009

The general rule about where to breathe when singing is to follow the punctuation of the song. Natural pause points in language (such as commas, colons, or periods) provide possible places for you to take a breath.

Of course, there are many exceptions to this rule, but take a song and try it on.

While neoclassical music sounds modern in many ways, it is written following the basic forms and ideals of the Classical period.

Monday

February

23

2009

Record yourself singing a challenging song. Notice your consonants, both beginning and ending. Do they sound natural or do they explode?

Pay special attention to the consonants T, D, P, and K.

"Music is moonlight in the gloomy night of life." - Jean Paul Richter

Note-A-Day Calendars

Sunday

November

8

2009

How easily does your voice move today? If it's slower than usual, work consistently, but don't push it too far or too fast.

Sing, then rest for a few minutes. Sing, then rest. A slow or tired voice will respond better with short rest periods.

The voice is considered to have at least four voice registers. Ranging from lowest to highest, they are the chest register, head register, falsetto, and whistle register.

Note-A-Day Calendars

Tuesday
February
24
2009

For a few minutes each, tone on these vowels: O, A, and E. Where do you feel the vibrations in your body? Expand the vibrations 360 degrees around you. Notice how this feels. Allow the vibrations to relax and energize you.

Variations of a round (where two or more voices sing the same melody starting at different times) include a catch (where a catch phrase is split between several voices) and a canon (where the voices begin the melody at different

Saturday
November
7
2009

To help with hydration, drink liquids with lemon juice or herbal teas. Throat drops with glycerin are also helpful, but avoid menthol and eucalyptus. They can be too drying.

"Give me a laundry list and I'll set it to music." - Gioacchino Antonio Rossini

Wednesday
February
25
2009

Another way to find the optimum pitch of your speaking voice is to simply count the numbers one through five. The natural pitch that your voice finds is your optimum speaking pitch.

If it's higher than your normal pitch, try to gradually adjust to this new pitch during the day by doing this exercise again. Do it every day, until you feel you've adjusted to this new pitch center.

The first record to sell one million copies was "Chattanooga Cho-Cho" by The Glen Miller Orchestra in 1942.

Friday
November
6
2009

Choose a genre of music that you enjoy and research its history. Schedule a time to visit a local art, history, or folk museum where you can learn more about the cultural context of this music.

A half-step is the distance from one key on the keyboard to the next adjacent key.

Note-A-Day Calendars

Thursday
February
26

2009

If your voice can move from pitch to pitch, you can exercise it. On the contrary, vocal rest is recommended for laryngitis (when there is no movement from pitch to pitch). However, if your voice has any movement between pitches, some easy, light exercises can help increase the blood flow to the vocal folds and surrounding tissues.

A "through-composed" song has new music for each stanza of a poem.

Thursday

November

5

2009

Improvise, as if your voice were different stringed instruments: when singing low, you are a double bass; when singing in the middle, you are a cello; when singing high, you are a violin.

The cantata is similar to the opera. Like the opera, it is a series of arias and recitatives, but it is not staged or acted.

Note-A-Day Calendars

Friday

February

27

2009

Sing a song you know well and be as vulnerable as possible. Singing is a vulnerable thing to do, and when we can connect the song to our heart, it makes it even more personal, more real, and more alive!

Take a few minutes to close your eyes and notice your breathing. Now focus on your heart, and notice your feelings at this moment. As you sing, allow your voice to come from this place deep within yourself.

In the 20th century, recording techniques became musical elements in their own right.

Note-A-Day Calendars

Wednesday
November
4
2009

Using your pitch pipe (see the preface) and starting with E as 1, play each group and listen carefully:

1 3 5 8
8 5 3 5 3 5 1
3 1 3 5 8 5 3 1
5 1 5 3 5 1 5 8

Next, go back and "think" (audiate) each group.

Soubrette, heldentenor, bass-baritone, coloratura, baritenor, and basso buffo are just some of the many designations for singers.

Note-A-Day Calendars

Saturday
February
28

2009

Looking at the Circle of Fifths in the preface, start with a C minor scale and name every note.

Test your memory as much as possible. Go through the G and D scales, making note of the ones you don't have memorized.

"Music is my religion." - Jimi Hendrix

Note-A-Day Calendars

Tuesday

November

3

2009

Look at any held note (over four counts) in a song you are singing. For this note to sound alive, you must crescendo or decrescendo as you sing. Otherwise, the note will sound like it's stagnating. Give all your long notes a new life today.

"I worry that the person who thought up muzak may be thinking up something else." - Lily Tomlin

Note-A-Day Calendars

Sunday

March

1

2009

Bring your voice into your everyday life as much as possible today. Sing as you shower, as you cook, as you drive or walk, and (if possible) as you work.

Make up melodies or lyrics or just sing gibberish. Notice how you feel at the end of the day!

Review your musical goals today.

Note-A-Day Calendars

Monday

November

2

2009

Listen to at least three different singers (you can go to a music store, or search online; sites like www.Amazon.com offer free samples).

Notice the differences between them, and what you like and don't like about each one.

Bryan Adams took a picture of the queen of England that was used on a Canadian stamp.

Monday
March
2
2009

Find a great local teacher and take a lesson or series of lessons from him or her (ask at a music store or local school for recommendations). Focus on vocal technique.

A galliard is a lively and vigorous sixteenth-century dance.

Note-A-Day Calendars

Sunday

November

1

2009

As you practice today, notice your posture.

Take a moment to stretch. Let your spine elongate upwards, your shoulders relax, your breathing be low in the belly, your knees free to move, your feet parallel and grounded.

Notice any places where you feel excess tension. Breathe into these area(s) and see if you can release some of the tension. Continue to notice and release during your practice time.

Review your musical goals today.

Note-A-Day Calendars

Tuesday
March
3
2009

Choose a song that you know well and want to sing or communicate at a deeper emotional level.

Write out one phrase of text, then leave a blank line below it.

In the blank line, write in your own subtext - any text that you feel communicates the emotion(s) that you want to convey. It could be related to the text, or not.

Do this for the entire song. Memorize both the text and the subtext.

There are six versions of Franz Schubert's "Die Forelle" ("The Trout") because when friends asked him for copies of the song, he wrote out new copies as best as he could remember at the time.

Note-A-Day Calendars

Saturday

October

31

2009

Singing is healing. Sometimes we resist singing because we're blocking emotions. Yet when we start, the energy of singing can quickly create emotional shifts that transform us.

Find a phrase or a song that reflects an emotion that you want to express, but feel blocked around expressing. Start singing, staying aware of and open to your feelings. Let yourself feel whatever is present for you.

"Great music completely obliterates any conceptions of genre." - Billy Corgan

Note-A-Day Calendars

Wednesday
March
4
2009

When we combine our voice with our intention, we can bring clarity and healing to our lives.

Begin with a brief physical warm-up. Find a comfortable place to sit. Sing one note as you experiment with moving the jaw, cheek muscles, tongue, and roof of the mouth.

As the sound enters the acoustical chambers of the pharynx, state your intention. Open your heart and tone.

End with silence, continuing to hold your intention.

"Music is the art which is most nigh to tears and memory." - Oscar Wilde

Note-A-Day Calendars

Friday

October

30

2009

Sing a piece of music that you're familiar with. Notice how you are breathing throughout the entire piece.

Notice if and how your breathing changes during specific parts. Do you need to adjust how often you breathe, or how much air you take in one breath?

Most singing involves shaping the voice to form words, but other types of voice instrumental music, such as scat singing and yodeling, use open sounds or nonsense syllables (vocables) instead.

Thursday
March
5
2009

Look up and memorize the definitions for the following terms (use www.8notes.com/glossary for a good resource): mezzo forte, moderato, obbligato, ostinato, and prestissimo.

The top selling singles of all time are Elton John's "Candle in the Wind '97" at 33 million units, Bing Crosby's "White Christmas" at 30 million, and Bill Haley's "Rock Around the Clock" at 25 million.

Thursday

October

29

2009

Sing a song you have memorized in three different ways: with your eyes looking around, with your eyes fixated on one thing, and with your eyes shut. Notice how shifting your eyes affects your singing.

Sing the song once more, shifting your eyes as you desire, but with increased awareness of how you are using them.

Throughout the Baroque period, composers were employed by the church and the wealthy ruling class.

Note-A-Day Calendars

Friday

March

6

2009

A well-trained voice can sing in a variety of different styles. Generally, classical styles emphasize a smooth vocal line. Pop styles focus on short phrases that stay connected. Strive to maintain a clear, expressive sound, no matter which style you are working with.

"The whole problem can be stated quite simply by asking, "Is there a meaning to music?" My answer would be, "Yes." "Can you state in so many words what the meaning is?" My answer to that would be, "No."" - Aaron Copland

Note-A-Day Calendars

Wednesday

October

28

2009

Do you have any of the following vocal symptoms?

•hoarseness
•fatigue (voice tires or changes quality after singing for a short period of time)
•loss of range (high? low?)
•breathiness
•tickling or choking sensation in the throat while singing
•pain in the throat while singing.

If so, consider consulting with a Singing Voice Specialist; see www.VoiceFoundation.org for more information.

"A cappella" is Italian for "as in chapel," meaning performed in the church style. It is choral singing without instrumental accompaniment.

Note-A-Day Calendars

Saturday

March

7

2009

Create a recording of inspirational singers and make a few copies for around the house and in the car. Listen to it periodically for inspiration.

Throughout The Beatles' career, Ringo received far more fan mail than any of the other members.

Tuesday

October

27

2009

If you are preparing for an upcoming performance, work on building your voice consistently up until the day of the performance. On the day of your performance, do your vocal exercises, but don't oversing. Shift the focus from "building up" to maintaining where you are, so that you can perform to the best of your ability.

The term "blue note," usually associated with the famous jazz record label, refers to the diminished fifth - the basic building-block interval of the blues.

Note-A-Day Calendars

Sunday

March

8

2009

Practice singing eight-tone scales, modifying your vowel (to a darker vowel) as you go up, and unmodifying it (to a brighter vowel) as you come down (e.g., start with oh, modify up to oo, modify back to oh).

Vowel modification will help to offset the natural tendency of your voice to be overly bright at higher pitches and overly dark at lower pitches.

While playing in front of a large lake at the Crystal Palace Bowl in London in 1970, Pink Floyd played so loud that a number of fish were killed.

Monday

October

26

2009

Write a simple song today: using a poem that you wrote or someone else's that you like, improvise with the text in a musical style that you enjoy. Tape yourself, and if you like some of it, keep it for later!

In sight-singing, solfege (or solmization) is a way of assigning syllables to the degrees or steps of the diatonic scale. In order, they are: Do, Re, Mi, Fa, So(l), La, Ti (or Si), and Do (for the octave).

Monday

March

9

2009

As the holidays draw closer, plan a time to gather with friends and family to honor the season with singing songs that you love.

Even one simple song together can create a wonderful feeling of warmth and openness. It's a busy season, but be proactive!

In jazz, a shake is a trill between one note and its minor third.

Note-A-Day Calendars

Sunday
October
25
2009

Before practicing, do a relaxation exercise (you might want to lie down).

Starting with your head and moving to your feet, tense and relax each part of your body, squeezing each part tightly, then breathing and releasing each part simultaneously.

See if you can maintain this relaxed alertness as you practice.

A toccata is a musical form designed to show off the instrument and the technique of the player.

Note-A-Day Calendars

Tuesday

March

10

2009

When you perform next, let yourself have the freedom to make mistakes.

Be accessible. Be YOU, not perfect. Your passion and authenticity will be remembered, far longer than your perfection. Besides, most of the mistakes that we notice go unnoticed by the audience!

"Figured bass" is a system of musical shorthand developed in the early Baroque period. It made keyboard parts easier to write.

Note-A-Day Calendars

Saturday

October

24

2009

Experiment with breathing more frequently as you sing a familiar phrase of a song. Try taking small, quick breaths during a longer phrase, instead of taking one large breath at the beginning and going until you are almost empty. It may feel strange at first, but when you learn to do it correctly, it will be easier for you and unnoticeable to others.

In atonal music, all twelve notes of the chromatic scale are used equally, and the rhythms are irregular and unpredictable.

Wednesday

March

11

2009

Your larynx is your voice box, housing the vocal folds and protecting the trachea. Using two fingers, find your larynx and gently move it from side to side. A child's larynx is 40% smaller than the average adult male larynx. A woman's larynx is 15% smaller than a man's.

As you sing today, notice the position of your larynx. Different vocal styles (and vocal colors) require the larynx to change position.

The term "disc jockey" was first used in 1935. It was coined by American commentator Walter Winchell, combining "disc" (referring to disc records) and "jockey" (an operator of a machine).

Friday

October

23

2009

Food affects our voice. Eating well impacts our energy level and ability to focus. Pay attention to the kinds of food you eat and how they affect your health and energy.

Notice how eating before you sing affects your energy and concentration, and how both change in response to the foods you are eating. Wait at least one hour after eating to practice so that your body won't be using energy to digest the food.

"Music expresses that which cannot be said, and on which it is impossible to be silent." - Victor Hugo

Thursday

March

12

2009

As you practice a song today, notice when it sounds/feels especially natural and "right."

Pause and try to memorize this sound/feeling. See if you can repeat it. This will help your mind access the information faster next time you sing it.

An apostrophe placed above the staff indicates to take a breath.

Note-A-Day Calendars

Thursday

October

22

2009

Sit outside and sing a song. Notice how being outside affects your singing.

The Jew's harp, or mouth harp, is thought to be one of the oldest musical instruments in the world; a musician playing it can be seen in a Chinese drawing from the 3rd century BC.

Friday

March

13

2009

Images such as “fake a yawn” or “fake a smile” are more of an artistic technique than a vocal technique. The foundation of solid technique lies with exercises that build strength and flexibility, then it continually returns to the clarity of vowels that you are singing. Are you singing the correct vowels?

A cadenza is a solo section in a concerto or similar work that is used to display the performer’s technique.

Note-A-Day Calendars

Wednesday

October

21

2009

Pauses within a song are important for the listener because it allows them to absorb the music and the text. Sing a song you know well, noticing each pause and the role it plays in the expression of the music. Let the pauses help you to relax and breathe deeply.

A jig, or gigue, is a baroque dance in a lively compound meter.

Note-A-Day Calendars

Saturday
March
14
2009

Perform at least one song for young children (under eight years old), either at a school or other similar setting. Don't choose anything that's too loud, or that you sense they wouldn't appreciate.

Tell them a little bit about yourself, why you like to sing, and what music you'll be singing.

A baritone is a male voice of intermediate pitch, between bass and tenor. It is typically written for in the range G one octave and a fourth below middle C to E above middle C, although it is often extended at the top.

Note-A-Day Calendars

Tuesday
October
20
2009

Choose a song you can sing well. If it's normally sung without amplification, use a microphone. If it's normally sung with a microphone, sing it without one.

Johann Sebastian Bach is considered by many to be the best composer of the Baroque period.

Sunday

March

15

2009

Important events in our lives shape who we are and how we express our deepest emotions.

Recall such an event, then choose a song (or improvise) that helps you express the depth of this experience. Create a safe space for yourself to sing, and feel, without judgment or expectation.

"Music is the medicine of the breaking heart." - Leigh Hunt

Note-A-Day Calendars

Monday
October
19
2009

Choose a song and find the highest note(s) in each phrase. As you sing, don't lift your chin or larynx up for the high note(s). Instead, practice singing just the vowels and modify them toward an "oh" or an "oo" as you are going up.

Pitch is determined by the sound's frequency of vibration. It refers to the relative highness or lowness of a tone. The greater the frequency, the higher the pitch.

Monday

March

16

2009

Looking at page 8, Spelling Scales and Chords, and page 10, the Circle of Fifths, spell an A# major scale (the notes are the same as Bb, but use sharps instead of flats).

"Life is like music; it must be composed by ear, feeling, and instinct, not by rule." - Samuel Butler

Sunday

October

18

2009

When preparing sheet music for an audition, be sure it is easy to read, well-marked (with any cuts you want), and in a 3-ring binder (not loose sheets). Create a binder for every audition you are ready to do, in case they want to hear something else.

In hardcore punk, hoarse shouting takes the place of singing, while in emo, some bands scream rather than sing. In metal, particularly the sub-genre of death metal, low growls called death grunts are favored over standard singing.

Tuesday

March

17

2009

The audience "listens" with their eyes 85% of the time. Remember this as you prepare for how you'll look and move during performance.

"Is it not strange that sheep's guts should hale souls out of men's bodies?"
- William Shakespeare

Note-A-Day Calendars

Saturday

October

17

2009

Create some simple flash cards that list different musical interpretations on each one, such as: fast, slow, loud, soft, staccato, legato, etc.

Sing a song you know well. Pick up a new flash card every 10-15 seconds and express the interpretation listed. Continue to play with this, keeping the ones you like, and discarding the rest.

"Music produces a kind of pleasure which human nature cannot do without."
- Confucius

Note-A-Day Calendars

Wednesday

March

18

2009

Find another musician (not a singer) to work with.

See what you can discover together. Improvise, write songs, share ideas, or whatever you like.

"In the strictest sense, [folk music] is music that is rarely written for profit. It's music that . . . has been passed down by oral tradition . . . [It] is participatory - you don't have to be a great musician to be a folk singer." - Gene Shay

Note-A-Day Calendars

Friday

October

16

2009

Notice your mental and physical state before you begin singing. Set an intention, a word or short phrase that determines how you would like to be in your session.

Write it down and refer to it occasionally throughout your session. When you're done practicing, notice how you've changed.

"Over the years I hope I've become more of a musician and less of a guitarist."
- Larry Coryell

Thursday

March

19

2009

Take a trip to your local library. Browse through the CD's and sheet music, looking for possible new material. Check out what interests you and don't hold back, since it's free!

Dolce means "sweetly."

Thursday

October

15

2009

Sing a G minor scale. Next, sing the syllables do (1), re (2), mi (3), fa (4), sol (5), la (6), ti (7), do (8), with each syllable corresponding to the note in the scale.

Next, play the root (first) note on your pitch pipe. Sing that note, then sing (without playing) the entire scale, ascending and descending.

"Without music, life is a journey through a desert." - Pat Conroy

Friday

March

20

2009

Finding the "rhythmic pocket" of the song is essential, no matter what style you are singing.

Record yourself singing a song with accompaniment. Listen to it. Are you singing in rhythm and in the correct style for the song? If not, sing along with a good professional recording until singing in the "pocket" becomes habitual. Record yourself again and listen.

Approximately one-third of recorded CDs are pirated.

Wednesday

October

14

2009

Consider subscribing to a music magazine or journal that you enjoy. Or, take a trip to your local library to find some that interest you.

"But enough joking. I am singing. This is all my life." - Placido Domingo

Note-A-Day Calendars

Saturday

March

21

2009

Sometimes, directors can be very demanding of singers. You always have the choice to "mark" (sing with half your voice) during rehearsals, so that you can save yourself for performances.

Be careful of overworking your voice. You are in charge. Pay attention to the signals your voice gives you.

The most famous composer of tone poems was Richard Strauss. His tone poems include "Don Juan" and "Der Rosenkavalier."

Note-A-Day Calendars

Tuesday

October

13

2009

Sing a D major scale using the syllables do (1), re (2), mi (3), fa (4), sol (5), la (6), ti (7), do (8), with each syllable corresponding to the note in the scale.

With your pitch pipe, play the root (first) note, then the second note. Sing both, using syllables do and re.

Play the root note, then the third note; sing both using do and mi.

Play the root note and the fourth note; sing both using do and fa.

Continue doing this for the whole scale, ascending and descending.

Con moto means "with motion."

Note-A-Day Calendars

Sunday

March

22

2009

Sing the following patterns in the keys of Ab and Db:

1 3 2 4 3 4 2 1
1 2 1 4 2 1
3 1 2 3 4 2 1
5 3 4 2 1 7 1

Sing them first using numbers, then using the names of the actual notes.

Sacred Harp (or Shape Note) Singing (a form of choral singing) emphasizes participation, not performance. The singers sit in an inward-facing square with the leader in the center, where the greatest volume and balance is heard.

Note-A-Day Calendars

Monday
October
12
2009

Create a realistic weekly practice schedule. Try it, be flexible, and make adjustments as needed.

Remember that 15-20 minutes of practice a day is all you need to maintain your vocal strength and agility.

In "responsorial chant," soloists sing in alternation with the choir.

Note-A-Day Calendars

Monday
March
23
2009

The tessitura of a song is the part of the vocal register where the majority of the notes of a melody or a voice part lie.

Look at each song you are singing and determine if the tessitura is correct for you. Some signs of singing in the wrong tessitura are: vocal strain or hoarseness, vocal fatigue, or loss of range.

Singing in the wrong tessitura can lead to vocal damage. If in doubt, consult a professional.

Rap, slang for conversation, was created by African-Americans in the mid 1970s. It features rhyming lyrics that are often improvised and chanted to musical accompaniment, which is often sampled from well-known songs.

Note-A-Day Calendars

Sunday

October

11

2009

Spend five minutes writing about how sharing your voice is a gift you give to the world. Your passion and talent are unique and need to be shared with others.

What do you offer and share through your voice? You might consider asking others how they are positively affected by your singing.

A ballad is a narrative poem, often of folk origin and intended to be sung, consisting of simple stanzas and usually having a refrain.

Tuesday
March
24
2009

Notice any limiting ideas and beliefs you have about your singing abilities or goals. Some examples include: “I'm not as good as so and so”, “I started singing too late in life to be any good”, “I'm not a natural musician”, “I can't make a living making music”, etc.

Write them down. Read through the list. Before each one, say, “I'm choosing to let go of this belief”. Then, shred, burn, or throw away the paper.

Repeat this practice regularly.

During the Renaissance, madrigals, or songs for small groups of voices without instruments, were the most popular form of secular music.

Saturday

October

10

2009

Your voice resonates in the pharynx (extending from the vocal folds up to the nasal cavities) and the mouth. Experiment with these different resonating chambers.

On any vowel, "place" your sound in the lower, middle, and upper pharynx. Explore different sounds, colors, and textures.

A mezzo-soprano is a female singer with a range usually extending from the A below middle C to the A two octaves above. Mezzo-sopranos generally have a darker (or richer) vocal tone than sopranos.

Wednesday

March

25

2009

Looking at the Circle of Fifths in the preface, start with an A minor scale and name every note.

Test your memory as much as possible. Go through the E and B scales, making note of the ones you don't have memorized.

A strophic song consists of several stanzas, with the same music for each stanza.

Note-A-Day Calendars

Friday

October

9

2009

Performing involves being a “triple power” - a singer, actor, and dancer.

If your singing is the strongest, take some acting and movement classes. If your acting is the strongest, take some singing and movement classes.

Be a “triple power” on the stage.

“Music is the vernacular of the human soul.” - Geoffrey Latham

Note-A-Day Calendars

Thursday

March

26

2009

Take a song that you can sing but have not yet memorized and memorize it.

One theory about the evolution of language suggests that the human voice developed first for singing, and only later for speech.

Note-A-Day Calendars

Thursday

October

8

2009

Practice singing the following intervals (an interval is the distance between two notes) in the keys of F, C, and G:

major ninth (M9); 7 steps; Example: F to G (one octave above)
major thirteenth (M13); 10 ½ steps; Example: F to D (one octave above)

On your pitch pipe, play the higher note, then the lower note. Sing both. Memorize the sound.

"When words leave off, music begins." - Heinrich Heine

Note-A-Day Calendars

Friday

March

27

2009

Sing a song you know well and focus on the timing of your breathing. It's important to take a breath just before you begin a phrase, but be careful not to take it too early or too late. If it's too early, then you'll hold your breath before you start. If it's too late, then you won't get enough breath to sing the phrase.

Ricercar is an instrumental genre of the Renaissance, meaning to "search out." Many ricercars served as a prelude to "search out" the key or mode of a following piece.

Note-A-Day Calendars

Wednesday
October
7

2009

After a vigorous practice or performance, wait a half an hour and then spend a few minutes doing a vocal “warm-down.” Gently sing a few exercises and do some vocal glides. This will help to reset your voice and allow it to slowly come back to “neutral.”

Billy Joel played piano on The Shangri-Las’ “Leader Of The Pack” (1964).

Note-A-Day Calendars

Saturday

March

28

2009

Practice singing the following intervals (an interval is the distance between two notes) in the keys of C, F, and G:

perfect fourth (P4); 2 ½ steps; Example: C to F, F to Bb, G to C
perfect fifth (P5); 3 ½ steps; Example: C to G, F to C, G to D

If necessary, use your pitch pipe (or other instrument) to help find the pitches as a reference.

"If you hit a wrong note, then make it right by what you play afterwards."
- Joe Pass

Note-A-Day Calendars

Tuesday

October

6

2009

Some musicians have overcome obstacles to become successful:

Andrea Bocelli, Stevie Wonder, Ray Charles: blind
Ludwig van Beethoven: deaf
Teddy Pendergrass: accident/paraplegic
Django Reinhardt: only two functional right-hand fingers
Jason Becker: Lou Gehrig's disease

The vocal folds (or vocal cords) vibrate, modulating the flow of air being expelled from the lungs while singing. They are composed of twin infoldings of mucous membrane stretched horizontally across the larynx (or voice box).

Note-A-Day Calendars

Sunday

March

29

2009

At night, turn off all of the lights in your practice space. In complete darkness, improvise.

A time signature in simple meter will always have a 2, 3, or 4 for the top number.

Monday
October
5

2009

The best way to learn how to safely "scream" (in any musical style) without damaging your voice is to learn to sing a classical aria. The physical and vocal strength required is the same for both.

Find a classical aria, and practice it regularly. Notice how this affects your voice. You can also check out "The Zen of Screaming" by Melissa Cross for more ideas.

Minor scales come in three forms: natural, melodic, and harmonic.

Note-A-Day Calendars

Monday

March

30

2009

Memorize two scales from the Circle of Fifths (see preface). Sing them in major and minor keys.

Singing makes all the sad people happy, because it is the voice of happiness.
- Zulu saying

Note-A-Day Calendars

Sunday

October

4

2009

Practice singing the following intervals (an interval is the distance between two notes) in the keys of Eb and Bb:

major sixth (M6); 4 ½ steps; Example: Eb to
major seventh (M7); 5 ½ steps; Example: Eb to B

On your pitch pipe, play the higher note, then the lower note. Sing both. Memorize the sound.

Global sales of pre-recorded music total more than $40 billion.

Note-A-Day Calendars

Tuesday

March

31

2009

Explore listening to new music that you are interested in singing and write down two or three songs you'd like to work on. Choose one to start on this week.

"Music is the literature of the heart; it commences where speech ends." - Alphonse de Lamartine

Note-A-Day Calendars

Saturday

October

3

2009

Choose a song you are learning or are interested in and research it.

Research the composer, when the song was written, inspiration, and/or meaning behind it, etc. See how much information you can come up with. Notice if this helps you feel more connected to the music.

The lambada, the famous "forbidden dance" supposedly from Brazil, is actually a Bolivian folk tune that was popularized by the French pop group Kaoma.

Wednesday

April

1

2009

If you're performing with a sound system, be sure the technician at the sound board clearly understands the sound you are looking for. Give yourself plenty of time to do sound checks to find the correct balance and get comfortable with the resonance of the venue. If needed, work closely with the technician to find the sound you want. Your performance depends upon it!

Review your musical goals today.

Friday

October

2

2009

Think about your vocal health. Your voice reflects your physical, mental, and emotional state.

Today, treat yourself with respect by eating, exercising, and practicing as if you had the "performance of a lifetime" to sing tonight.

"Program music" is instrumental music associated with a story or idea.

Note-A-Day Calendars

Thursday

April

2

2009

If you're working towards an audition, remember to choose literature that reflects the depth and variety of your performing talents. You'll want to be prepared for any musical theatre audition with a ballad, an up-tempo piece, and a character piece.

Melisma is the technique of changing the pitch of a syllable of text while it is being sung. Music sung in this style is referred to as melismatic, as opposed to syllabic, where each syllable of text is matched to a single note.

Thursday

October

1

2009

On the Internet, research the anatomy of the larynx and the vocal folds.

Find a diagram and study it for a few minutes. Notice how complex this area of your body is, and how many different nerves, bones, and muscles are interconnected.

Review your musical goals today.

Note-A-Day Calendars

Friday

April

3

2009

Balanced registration is similar to the shape of a triangle.

The base of the triangle is your lower register. If the base it too small (tight, pinched, strained, overly bright or light), the middle and top will be diminished.

If the base is too wide (fuzzy, unfocused, overly dark and heavy), the voice will be too heavy all the way up and the top won't work well.

If the base is correct (focused, clear, clean, and ringing), the middle and top will be balanced and the voice will move easily from low to high.

Opera developed during the Baroque period, and infused music with the drama of storytelling.

Wednesday

September

30

2009

Sing with "vocal glides," swooping from low to high and back to low in your voice.

Notice the transition. Does your voice "grab" at the transition, or can you move smoothly from low to high? Glide as much as possible.

Doloroso means "sorrowfully."

Note-A-Day Calendars

Saturday

April

4

2009

Take a few minutes to write about your musical lineage. Were your parents or grandparents musicians? Did they influence your musical likes and dislikes?

How can you expand beyond any musical limits they may have set upon you?

"For me, singing is a way of escaping. It's another world. I'm no longer on earth." - Edith Piaf

Tuesday

September

29

2009

When first working on extending your upper register and developing high notes, they may be unfocused, too big or "blown out." To offset this tendency, allow your high notes to be smaller on top, as if they were tapering up to the top of a triangle.

"Klangfarbenmelodie" refers to distributing the notes of a melody amongst different instruments.

Sunday

April

5

2009

During an audition, if you have a bad start to a song, start again. This will not reflect negatively on you, and you will feel much better about your performance.

A grand piano can be played faster than an upright (spinet) piano.

Monday
September
28
2009

Expressive singing requires powerful energy.

Once you are vocally and physically warmed up, watch yourself in the mirror and sing a song that requires you to express strong emotions. Is your voice, body, face, and overall energy communicating what you are feeling?

If not, go back to your warm-ups and put more energy into them. Then, sing the song again.

The chest voice, which produces the sensation of the sound coming from the upper chest, is the register typically used in everyday speech. Being a lower frequency sound, it resonates mostly in the larger cavity of the chest.

Note-A-Day Calendars

Monday

April

6

2009

Quality of practice yields more results than quantity. Fifteen minutes of focused practicing is more effective than one hour of distracted singing. Make sure you are in a space where you are completely uninterrupted from phones, children, TVs, etc., and stay focused on your music.

Shock rocker Alice Cooper was once elected homecoming queen for the University Of Houston.

Note-A-Day Calendars

Sunday
September
27
2009

Today, sing with different variations of vocal timbre. Take one phrase of a song, and sing it three ways: with a "pop" sound, a "musical theatre" sound, and an "operatic" sound.

Which timbre do you like the best with this phrase? Be sure to sing the appropriate color line with each song you choose.

Barry Manilow's 1976 chart-topping song "I Write the Songs" was not written by him (it was actually written by Bruce Johnston of the Beach Boys).

Note-A-Day Calendars

Tuesday

April

7

2009

Reflect back on your experience as a singer. As you've grown older, has your voice changed in its ability to warm-up? When you're younger, it can take less time to warm-up, but your voice won't have as much stamina. As you grow older, it can take more time to warm up, but your voice will have more stamina. Remember that as your voice changes, it is not worsening, it's just part of aging.

"There is no truer truth obtainable by Man than comes of music." - Robert Browning

Note-A-Day Calendars

Saturday

September

26

2009

When working with live accompaniment, be clear about the tempo that you want for each song. Unless the style has rubato (variations in tempo within a phrase), be consistent in your tempo.

If you rush or drag, try to determine why you're doing it. Do you have enough time to breathe? Are your consonants coming just before the beat so the vowel is on the beat?

Make any necessary adjustments, and repeat the song.

Meter is the regular recurring pattern of strong and weak beats of equal duration, also known as time.

Note-A-Day Calendars

Wednesday

April

8

2009

Gather your family and/or friends and perform for them (even if it's only one or two people). Sing at least one song you enjoy.

Before starting, talk briefly about what you're going to sing. When you are completely finished, thank and acknowledge your audience.

The whistle register, comprising of the highest notes that a human voice can reach, is also often considered a "full" register, although the ability to use it well is rare.

Friday

September

25

2009

Record yourself singing a song that you are working on.

As you listen, pay close attention to the beginning (onset) and ending (release) of each note.

Is the onset clean, without any extra noise? Is the release clean, without any added accent?

Record the sections that need work again, using the recording to give you feedback and make necessary adjustments.

To earn a gold disc, an album needs to sell 100,000 copies in Britain, and 500,000 in the United States.

Note-A-Day Calendars

Thursday

April

9

2009

Sing a G major scale using the syllables do (1), re (2), mi (3), fa (4), sol (5), la (6), ti (7), do (8), with each syllable corresponding to the note in the scale.

With your pitch pipe, play the root (first) note, then the second note. Sing both, using syllables do and re.

Play the root note, then the third note; sing both using do and mi.

Play the root note and the fourth note; sing both using do and fa.

Continue doing this for the whole scale, ascending and descending.

A "song cycle" is a group of songs connected by a unifying idea or story.

Note-A-Day Calendars

Thursday

September

24

2009

If you are having consistent vocal problems, consider seeing a chiropractor or osteopath. The alignment of cervical vertebrae directly affects vocal fold function.

There was one emotional outlet my people always had when they had the blues. That was singing. - Ethel Waters

Note-A-Day Calendars

Friday

April

10

2009

Take a song that you are working on. Try to hear the entire piece of music in your head.

This process is called audiation, and is the basis for all musical learning.

"I just wanted a song to sing, and there came a point where I couldn't sing anything . . . nobody else was writing what I wanted to sing. I couldn't find it anywhere. If I could I probably would never have started writing." – Bob Dylan

Note-A-Day Calendars

Wednesday
September
23
2009

Looking in a full-length mirror, sing a song you have memorized and notice the gestures you use.

Stretch your arms and shoulders, then sing it again, using silly, "unrealistic" gestures.

Sing it one more time, and incorporate some new gestures to find which ones are more "natural" for you.

Isorhythm occurs when parts of a melody are placed in a repeated pattern in a polyphonic work.

Note-A-Day Calendars

Saturday
April
11
2009

It's been said that music is the space between the notes. Today, pay particular attention to the space between all the notes you sing.

Much of the Lutheran church music of the seventeenth and eighteenth centuries was an outgrowth of the chorale.

Tuesday

September

22

2009

Record yourself singing a song, then evaluate how “natural” it is. Are the words clear, without compromising the phrasing or style? If not, sing the song a bit softer, focusing on clarity of articulation.

Sing it again, adding a bit more volume, while trying to maintain the same clarity.

Prior to his fame, Axl Rose earned $8 an hour for smoking cigarettes for a science experiment at UCLA.

Note-A-Day Calendars

Sunday

April

12

2009

Use your pitch pipe or instrument to play a D. Sing the major third and perfect fifth above it (F# and A, respectively). Then the minor third and perfect fifth (F and A, respectively).

Do this with each note in the D major scale.

"Singing instrumental music is most important because, while you play an instrument, you are singing through the instrument . . . actually, you are singing inside." - Ali Akbar Khan

Note-A-Day Calendars

Monday
September
21
2009

As you review your musical goals today, think about your purpose in life. How does singing help you express this purpose?

A symphony is a long composition for orchestra, usually with three to four movements.

Note-A-Day Calendars

Monday
April
13
2009

Sing the following patterns in the keys of G minor and D minor:

1 3 2 4 3 4 2 1
1 2 1 4 2 1
3 1 2 3 4 2 1
5 3 4 2 1 7 1

Sing first using numbers, then using the names of the actual notes.

The word "guitar" probably comes from the word "kithara," which was the principal stringed instrument of the ancient Greeks, and later of the Romans.

Note-A-Day Calendars

Sunday

September

20

2009

When working with a new piece, listen closely to the accompaniment (live or recorded). The first few times, focus solely on the accompaniment, tuning out the vocal. Learn its different textures and nuances; they have a lot to do with the mood and energy of the song.

Next, listen to both the accompaniment and the vocal. Notice how your vocal part is a duet with it.

Composers of the late 18th century became fascinated with the new possibilities of symphonic and other instrumental music, and generally neglected choral music.

Note-A-Day Calendars

Tuesday
April
14

2009

The essential components of music are tone (quality of sound or timbre, e.g., a trombone compared to a harp), pitch (how high or low a note is), rhythm (grouping and accentuation of notes), and dynamics (loud vs. soft).

Choose one note and experiment with each of the four components.

"Just as certain selections of music will nourish your physical body and your emotional layer, so other musical works will bring greater health to your mind."
- Hal A. Lingerman

Note-A-Day Calendars

Saturday

September

19

2009

Studies have shown that teachers remember more from their classes than their students! Plus, teaching something, no matter how small, builds confidence.

Teach someone you know something that you've learned about singing.

A slur is a curved line either above or below notes. It connects two pitches that are to be played smoothly.

Note-A-Day Calendars

Wednesday
April
15
2009

Choose a song you can sing well. Sing it in different styles, such as rock, reggae, blues, jazz, Latin, funk, punk, new age, classical, etc.

“The high note is not the only thing.” - Placido Domingo

Note-A-Day Calendars

Friday

September

18

2009

The more a phrase jumps around, the more you need to pick out key words and syllables to focus on.

Start by singing the phrase on “la”, checking for the correct notes and rhythms. Then speak the words of the phrase, noticing which syllables you naturally emphasize more.

Sing the phrase with the words, emphasizing those same syllables.

Grazioso means “gracefully.”

Thursday

April

16

2009

Create a five-minute physical warm-up routine to do before you start singing.

Start with feet, ankles, legs, etc., working your way up the spine. Finish with gentle shoulder and neck stretches. Massage any tight areas. Breathe.

Enjoy the openness that you feel.

"I'm used to singing in churches where no one would dare stop me until the Lord arrives!" - Mahalia Jackson

Note-A-Day Calendars

Thursday
September
17

2009

This is the shortest day of the year: sing a song (or improvise a song) that honors the return of the light.

"Some fans demonstrate their enthusiasm with bone-crushing hand shakes. My former teacher, Julian Bream, often bows Japanese-style with his hands behind his back. Smart man!" - Liona Boyd

Friday

April

17

2009

Hearing is a physical process. Listening is a mental process.

Record yourself singing anything. Listen to it with complete attention, find one or two items to change, then sing it again. The more you listen, the more you'll learn.

"I can't talk about my singing. I'm inside it. How can you talk about something you're inside of?" – Janis Joplin

Note-A-Day Calendars

Wednesday

September

16

2009

Trust your musical instincts. This will lead you to finding your own musical expression in the world.

You can consult others for their expertise, but always return to your own musical instincts.

An alto or contralto, referring to the deepest female (or highest male) voice, has a range from the F below middle C to the E a tenth above. At the bottom of their range, altos sound almost like tenors.

Note-A-Day Calendars

Saturday

April

18

2009

Improvise today with a friend.

Ask your roommate, spouse, child, or friend to join you for a few minutes. Pretend to have a conversation using sounds (any sounds at all), but not words.

Keep it simple and silly and you'll both be laughing!

A movement is a self-contained section of a larger composition.

Tuesday
September
15

2009

The higher the note you sing, the lower the breath needs to be in the torso. Focus on your support today.

"Music has been my playmate, my lover, and my crying towel." - Buffy Sainte-Marie

Sunday
April
19

2009

Today, practice singing in front of a mirror. In addition to your vocal ability, your body language is part of the package you present.

Practice with different ways of standing, sitting, other postures, or gestures. Find what makes your body as loose and comfortable as possible.

How comfortable you are in front of a mirror will reflect on how comfortable you'll be in front of an audience.

Berlioz used the term "idee fixe" to describe a recurring theme in a piece of music.

Note-A-Day Calendars

Monday

September

14

2009

Recall your past performances, or, if you've never performed, what you imagine performing would be like.

Think back to (or imagine) the best performance. How did you feel? What did you sing? What were the circumstances and conditions, such as location, audience size and demographics, temperature, atmosphere, etc.?

Picture it with as much detail as possible, and notice how your body feels. Stay with this feeling for a few minutes. Relish in it.

In "chance music," the composer leaves a lot up to the performer. As a result, each performance tends to be different.

Monday

April

20

2009

Vibrato is the natural oscillation of the vocal folds. You will know your vibrato is correct when you can move smoothly (legato) from pitch to pitch. Try singing a classical piece that has some rapidly moving passages. How well does your voice move?

In the old South, the singing of working men set the rhythm of the work. Being hired to work in any of the laborer's gangs depended on whether or not a man could sing.

Note-A-Day Calendars

Sunday

September

13

2009

The vocal folds are one-third cartilaginous (made up of cartilage, a somewhat elastic tissue) and two-thirds membranous (a thin, pliable layer of tissue). Nodules can form only on the membranous layers of the folds.

If you take aspirin regularly and have nodules or polyps, consult an ear, nose and throat specialist (ENT) first. Aspirin can thin the blood too much, leading to other possible health risks for singers in this situation.

James Brown's wife tried to get her traffic tickets dismissed because of "diplomatic immunity," claiming that her husband is the official "ambassador of soul." She lost the case.

Note-A-Day Calendars

Tuesday

April

21

2009

Looking at page 8 in the preface, Spelling Scales and Chords, and page 10, the Circle of Fifths, spell a D# major scale (the notes are the same as Eb, but use sharps instead of flats).

"Music is the medicine of the mind." - John A. Logan

Note-A-Day Calendars

Saturday

September

12

2009

Notice how you feel as you sing today. Does your body feel connected to the music? What emotions are you aware of? What sensations are you aware of? Are you thinking about what you're singing, feeling it, or both?

Rather than going for perfection in your singing today, see how connected you can feel to what you're singing.

Some types of vocal ensembles include trios, quartets (e.g., barbershop quartets), quintets, vocal groups, singing groups, choirs (with eight or more singers and doubled parts), and choruses (with many singers on each part).

Wednesday

April

22

2009

Find a four-part song (soprano, alto, tenor, and bass) and sight-read a part other than your own (sopranos, sing the alto part; tenors sing the baritone or bass part, etc.).

The world's largest disco, consisting of 13,000 people, was held at the Buffalo Convention Center in New York in 1979, earning a place in the Guinness Book of World Records.

Note-A-Day Calendars

Friday
September
11

2009

Pick a date to go hear a professional singer perform. Some places to check for upcoming concerts include local or independently-local newspapers, college campuses, coffeehouses, music stores, stadiums, arenas, and recital halls. You can also inquire at a local music store about any good singers who will be performing in the area.

Chuck Berry holds a degree in cosmetology.

Thursday

April

23

2009

Listen to a style of vocal music that you are not familiar with. Notice the instruments and how they interact with the voices.

What makes this style unique? How does it make you feel? See if you can remain open and curious as you listen to it.

Resolution is the conclusion of a musical idea.

Thursday

September

10

2009

Record yourself singing a song that you are working on. Listen to it, and, as objectively as possible, critique your singing (both positives and negatives). It might help to imagine that you are listening to someone else.

Use these observations to improve.

A grace note is an ornamental note, often printed in small type and not performed rhythmically.

Friday

April

24

2009

English is one of the hardest languages to sing in because there are over 108 different vowel combinations (because of diphthongs - see May 8th). Consider singing a song in Italian, Spanish, French, German, or another language. Consult a vocal coach as needed.

Many Appalachian folk ballads, such as "Barbara Allen," are variations of traditional songs from the British Isles.

Note-A-Day Calendars

Wednesday

September

9

2009

To help your rib cage stay lifted during singing, tie a stretchy band or cloth around your torso, close to the bottom of your rib cage. Make it fit snugly, but not too tightly, so that you notice the pressure against your ribs.

Keep this on during the first half of your practice session, then take it off and see if you can maintain the lift in the rib cage through each phrase that you sing.

Range is the distance between the lowest and highest notes of a melody.

Note-A-Day Calendars

Saturday

April

25

2009

Look at the literature you're working on right now. The tessitura for female tunes goes up and down continuously. The tessitura for high male tunes (tenor) goes up and stays up.

If you're a woman singing male tunes, it could lead to vocal strain since the tessitura is too consistently high. Choose wisely, since your vocal health depends on it.

During the Renaissance, the rise of music printing encouraged the spread of instrumental music for amateurs.

Tuesday

September

8

2009

Find a rhythm instrument (this could be a plastic container from your kitchen) that you can use to accompany yourself. Create a simple rhythm and improvise along with it, letting go of your notions of a "right" or "wrong" sound.

Explore new and strange sounds. Get creative! How do you feel?

"Spem in alium," composed ca. 1570, is a 40-part motet by Thomas Tallis for eight choirs of five voices each.

Sunday
April
26
2009

Spend five minutes writing about how you would like to grow artistically. Consider working with a professional, either individually or in a group, to move you towards your musical goals.

Overtures appeared throughout the Baroque and Classical periods as instrumental introductions to operas in order to set a particular mood or atmosphere.

Monday
September
7

2009

If you don't have any performances lined up for the holidays, think about what you might like to do. Sing a song for friends or family? Sing at an open mic? Go carolling? Perform in a musical?

Use this time to set some performing goals.

"Rhythmic serialism" is a compositional technique based on a fixed pattern of different note lengths.

Note-A-Day Calendars

Monday

April

27

2009

Sing the following patterns in the keys of E minor and B minor:

1 3 2 4 3 4 2 1

1 2 1 4 2 1

3 1 2 3 4 2 1

5 3 4 2 1 7 1

Sing first using numbers, then using the names of the actual notes.

More than 2,500 cover versions of The Beatles' "Yesterday" exist, making it the most recorded song in history.

Note-A-Day Calendars

Sunday
September
6
2009

Create your own pentatonic (five note) scale.
Improvise with it, and/or create a song.

"If you can walk, you can dance. If you can talk, you can sing." - Zimbabwe proverb

Note-A-Day Calendars

Tuesday

April

28

2009

Practice singing the following intervals (an interval is the distance between two notes) in the keys of D and A:

major second (M2); 1 step; Example: D to E
major third (M3); 2 steps; Example: D to F#

On your pitch pipe, play the higher note, then the lower note. Think both. Sing both. Memorize the sound.

Physical tiredness shows in the voice: if you're fatigued, your vocal chords will be too, and you'll be more liable to vocal strain. Get plenty of rest!

Saturday

September

5

2009

Just before performing, here are some things you can do to help manage your nerves: check in with your body, do a relaxation or visualization exercise, pant like a dog (then take a deep breath), shake your hands violently, and do some slow, deep breathing.

The term "lieder" is the plural form of the German word "lied," which means "song." The function of lieder is to set fine poetry to beautiful music.

Note-A-Day Calendars

Wednesday

April

29

2009

Familiarize yourself with the Circle of Fifths (see preface). Starting from C major, memorize the order of the sharps and the order of the flats as you move clockwise and counterclockwise, respectively.

Gregorian chant was sung in the early Catholic church. In general, the chants were taught orally.

Friday

September

4

2009

Before you sing today, put on one of your favorite dance songs and dance around the room! Get into it - feel the power of your body as you move, sweat, and breathe.

Notice how your body feels, and how this affects your singing.

Piano accompaniment is often used for rehearsals, including a cappella music, even when different instrumentation is planned for performance.

Note-A-Day Calendars

Thursday

April

30

2009

Looking at page 8 in the preface, Spelling Scales and Chords, and page 10, the Circle of Fifths, spell a G# major scale (the notes are the same as Ab, but use sharps instead of flats).

Michael Jackson's "Billie Jean" was the first video by a black artist to air on MTV.

Thursday

September

3

2009

When singing with a microphone, practice holding it so that you feel relaxed in your hand, wrist, and arm. Use your grip to help you express yourself emotionally (i.e., a tight grip for expressing anger or an open grip for expressing love). Generally, keep the microphone one to two inches from your mouth (with variations for different vocal effects).

"Music is the language of the spirit. It opens the secret of life bringing peace, abolishing strife." - Kahlil Gibran

Note-A-Day Calendars

Friday

May

1

2009

Experiment with movement as you sing today. Put on some clothes that you are comfortable moving in. Start your session with stretching and vocalizing any sounds you want while you stretch.

During your practice, move freely while you sing. Don't hold back! Your voice will reflect the openness and spontaneity of your body.

Review your musical goals today.

Wednesday

September

2

2009

Find the autobiography of a singer you adore. Read some of it each day, even if it's just one page.

In 1987, Aretha Franklin, the "Queen of Soul," was the first female artist to be inducted into the "Rock 'n' Roll Hall of Fame." The Supremes followed in 1988.

Note-A-Day Calendars

Saturday

May

2

2009

To increase the expressiveness of a specific phrase, practice singing it with "clipped" notes (shorten the note value of every note so that it is almost spoken), then just speak the phrase.

Move back and forth between these two variations. Sing the phrase again and notice any changes you've made.

Troubadours were aristocratic poet-musicians of the Middle Ages.

Note-A-Day Calendars

Tuesday

September

1

2009

Return to a piece of music you learned in the past month and sing it again. Notice how much learning you retained.

Return to this song (or any new step in your learning) at irregular intervals throughout the year. This is a powerful way to reinforce your learning.

Review your musical goals today.

Sunday

May

3

2009

Journal for at least five minutes on your inspirations and aspirations for singing.

What or who inspired you to sing? Do you have any dreams related to singing?

Return to your journal periodically, simply to reflect or to update what you've written.

"I consider myself as a singer first, but something that really helped me come into my own is that there's not a separation between me singing and me playing the guitar. The two feed off each other." - Shawn Colvin

Monday

August

31

2009

Choose a movie to watch tonight that is somehow connected to singing. It could be a documentary, a concert recording, a musical, a drama, etc. Write about how it inspires you to be an artist.

The singing of the syllables do, re, mi, etc. is called solfege.

Note-A-Day Calendars

Monday

May

4

2009

Make a list of the things you want to practice today. Include how much time you wish to spend on each area. Notice if this helps you to stay more focused.

"There's a fine line between genius and insanity. I have erased this line."- Oscar Lavant

Note-A-Day Calendars

Sunday
August
30
2009

Review the "Three Areas" from the preface.

With a song you know well, experiment first with singing OOPS (the One and Only Perfect Sound), then singing UBU (Ugly But Useful sounds).

Start with the extremes of each. Slowly, begin moving between the two extremes, creating new blends of the two. You may arrive at choices you would like to use in performance.

Choral music was one of the only types of music to survive intact for the first 1000 years of Western music.

Note-A-Day Calendars

Tuesday

May

5

2009

Practice writing the following notes:
whole-note; half-note; quarter-note; eighth-note; sixteenth-note.
Write each at least five times.

Pink Floyd were the first band to use a quadraphonic sound system at their concerts. It used four different channels of audio, and was an early version of surround sound.

Saturday

August

29

2009

Choose a minor scale. While playing the scale on another instrument (or alternating with the pitch pipe), sing the note that is four notes above the one you are playing (while staying in the scale). Tip: first play the note you'll be singing to learn the pitch, then go back and play the first note while singing the second one.

Vertical sonority, otherwise known as harmony, considers the relationships between pitches that occur together or in succession.

Wednesday

May

6

2009

When singing with the greatest emotional output, don't thrust your chin forward. This compromises your posture and cramps the larynx.

Practice standing against a wall at these moments. Think "wall".

"There is something suspicious about music, gentlemen. I insist that she is, by her nature, equivocal. I shall not be going too far in saying at once that she is politically suspect." - Thomas Mann

Note-A-Day Calendars

Friday

August

28

2009

When introducing yourself and your song(s) at an audition:

•Choose a personality, such as charming, charismatic, etc., that you want to portray and embody that presence on stage

•Smile, say hello, and make eye contact with the people before starting (you don't have to look at them while you sing)

•Practice speaking with clarity and confidence, making sure that the end of your sentences don't go down in pitch

•Rehearse each introduction

A suite is a piece consisting of a series of dances.

Thursday

May

7

2009

When drinking water, don't "sip" throughout the day. Instead, drink 12-20 ounces all at once. In the mornings, it's especially important to hydrate yourself.

Remember that it takes two-three hours for liquid to absorb into your tissues, including your vocal folds. Drink plenty of water well in advance of any practice or performance.

The open-throat singing in parts of eastern Europe enables the singer to immensely project. Although called "open throat," the technique actually requires rigidity of the vocal chords.

Note-A-Day Calendars

Thursday
August
27

2009

To sing with correct support is key in developing your voice to its fullest potential. Be sure you're lifting inwards and upwards from as low as possible (below your belly button) with the abdominal bulk. If you lift up too high, it can lock the diaphragm.

The British are the highest per capita spenders on music, totaling 7.2 percent of the world music market.

Note-A-Day Calendars

Friday

May

8

2009

Take a moment before you start to loosen up your facial muscles. Keeping the lower half of your face still, express "surprise" with the upper half. Repeat.

Now switch, keeping the upper half still and expressing "surprise" with the lower half. Repeat.

Do this with happy, sad, angry,and joyful.

"I would advise you to keep your overhead down; avoid a major drug habit; play every day, and take it in front of other people. They need to hear it and you need them to hear it." - James Taylor

Wednesday

August

26

2009

At your next performance (or practice), notice what messages you give yourself before, during, and after you sing. Do they add to your nervousness or build your confidence?

Write any insights you have in your journal.

The first pop video was "Bohemian Rhapsody" by Queen, released in 1975.

Note-A-Day Calendars

Saturday

May

9

2009

While you sing a song, hold either side of your rib cage with your hands. Notice if it collapses inward as you sing.

Sing the song again, trying to hold your rib cage in an expanded state while you press both hands gently inward against your ribs.

Try this anytime you practice. It will help you to strengthen your support system.

Music for piano flourished throughout the Romantic period.

Tuesday

August

25

2009

Spend at least five minutes writing about your perception of your speaking voice. In our culture, women tend to “masculinize” their voices due to societal acceptance of commanding, louder voices (usually male). Men can feel vocally limited, due to this same standard.

What is your experience? Is there anything you’d like to change about your speaking voice?

“The pause is as important as the note.” - Truman Fisher

Note-A-Day Calendars

Sunday

May

10

2009

Like any athletic endeavor, singing exercises muscles that gain strength over time. To maintain this strength, establish a consistent practice schedule using the same vocal exercises each time. This could include vocal glides, five tone scales, eight tone scales, arpeggios (both legato and staccato) and any other exercises that your teacher recommends.

Write out your routine so you can remember it each day.

"You must feel what you're singing, not just have a good presentation of the language." - Cecilia Bartoli

Note-A-Day Calendars

Monday
August
24
2009

Before a performance, never apologize to your audience or adjudicators for your voice. Even if you know you're only at 50% of your usual level, chances are they won't recognize this. If you point it out in advance, it will draw their attention to any slight mistake that you make.

Perform to the best of your ability, and afterwards assess the positives that you noticed, not the negatives.

The first evidence of performance with more than one singer per part was in 1420 in the Old Hall Manuscript, in which there is occasional divisi (where one part divides into two different notes, obviously impossible for a soloist).

Monday

May

11

2009

Find a new piece of music and sight-read the rhythms, clapping on the beat (the steady tempo, not the pattern) and speaking the rhythmic pattern. Try this with and without a metronome.

Verisimo is a realistic and sensational type of late Romantic-era opera.

Note-A-Day Calendars

Sunday

August

23

2009

Choose a section of a song that has challenging jumps in it. Singing an "oo," slide from the lower note to the higher note, over and over again. Then slide from the higher note to the lower note, over and over again. Now sing the entire phrase, with words, and notice the difference.

"Music should never be harmless." - Robbie Robertson

Note-A-Day Calendars

Tuesday

May

12

2009

Prior to an important performance, build up your experience.

First, sing the song(s) for your friends, then for your family, then sing for a small group gathering, etc.

Each time you perform, make some notes in your journal about how you felt, what worked, and what didn't work.

Monophonic music uses only one note at a time, while polyphonic uses two or more.

Saturday

August

22

2009

Research the singer's role in each of the five main eras of classical music (Renaissance, Baroque, Classical, Romantic, and Modern).

Bob Dylan's first professional performance was as an opening act for John Lee Hooker at Gerde's Folk City in New York in 1961.

Note-A-Day Calendars

Wednesday

May

13

2009

Practice singing the following intervals (an interval is the distance between two notes) in the keys of E minor and B minor:

minor sixth (m6); 4 steps; Example: E to C
minor seventh (m7); 5 steps; Example: E to D

On your pitch pipe, play the higher note, then the lower note. Sing both. Memorize the sound.

The first CD pressed in the United States for commercial release was Bruce Springsteen's "Born in the USA."

Note-A-Day Calendars

Friday

August

21

2009

Write out the lyrics of one of the songs you're trying to memorize, as if it were a poem. Read through the "poem" at various times during the day: when you're eating, when you're waiting in line, before you go to bed, etc.

Antiphony is a style in which two or more choirs alternate with one another.

Note-A-Day Calendars

Thursday

May

14

2009

To sing well, you must have enough torso strength to support the sound. Do physical exercises to improve your torso strength.

The middle voice, also known as the "blend," describes the range of notes that mark the crossover between the chest and head (or falsetto) voice. Singers can choose whether to sing notes in this range in the head or chest voice.

Note-A-Day Calendars

Thursday

August

20

2009

Form a casual performing group for yourself. Meet once a month (or whatever works best for everyone) and sing for each other.

Decide whether or not you want to give and receive feedback. Enjoy the support of your musical community.

Although madrigals were initially dramatic settings of love poetry or mythological stories in Italy, they were eventually merged with the more upbeat balletto, celebrating often-silly songs of spring, or eating and drinking.

Note-A-Day Calendars

Friday

May

15

2009

Today, take yourself out to experience something fun and "artistic" around town. Perhaps there's a new gallery you've wanted to see, or a museum, or music store?

Follow your intuition. What feeds your inner artist today?

When you return, sing a song, reflecting on your experience as you sing.

"Leaders must encourage their organizations to dance to forms of music yet to be heard." - Warren G. Bennis

Note-A-Day Calendars

Wednesday

August

19

2009

How is your overall vocal health? Do you have any recurring health issues that are affecting your voice and need to be addressed?

If so, make a plan of action as to how this will happen. Be proactive.

Composers like Johann Sebastian Bach reacted to the Baroque trend of fancy ornamentation by creating complex polyphonic music consisting of elaborate melodies layered top of each other.

Saturday

May

16

2009

The male larynx is approximately 20% longer than the female larynx.

Male vocal folds grow at an average rate of seven mm per year. Female vocal folds grow at an average rate of four mm per year.

Changes in your voice are inevitable. Welcome them!

Homophony is a musical texture of numerous musical lines that involves only one melody of real interest.

Note-A-Day Calendars

Tuesday

August

18

2009

Look up and memorize definitions and/or notations for the following terms (www.8notes.com/glossary is a good resource): a tempo, andante, cadenza, coda, da capo (D.C.) .

The most important Classical era composers were Wolfgang Amadeus Mozart, Franz Joseph Haydn, and Ludwig van Beethoven.

Sunday

May

17

2009

Using your pitch pipe (see the preface), starting with D as 1, listen carefully as you play 1 3 5 8; immediately reproduce the sounds mentally (i.e., think them).

Play 1 5 8. Play 1 3 5 8 again.

Think 8. Think 5.

Sing 1. Test it.

Sing 3. Test it.

Play 1 8 5 3 1. Think 5.

Sing 3. Test it.

Sing 1. Test it.

The most famous composers of impressionist music were Claude Debussy and Maurice Ravel.

Note-A-Day Calendars

Monday

August

17

2009

Choose another genre of music you enjoy and research its history. Look on the Internet, or go to your local library or bookstore to find good resources.

Johann Stamitz expanded the orchestral score, making the winds essential for the composition. He was also one of the first composers to give independent lines to oboes.

Note-A-Day Calendars

Monday

May

18

2009

One way to help manage the nerves of performing is to construct an audience in your mind (practice this at home first). Who are the people that love and adore you, no matter what you do?

Place them in the hall. Keep their name(s) in mind as you see their faces smiling at you.

Sing through a song, keeping this image in your mind's eye. Repeat this several times, making the images, sounds, colors, textures, etc. as vivid as possible.

A bass (or basso in Italian) is a male singer who sings in the lowest vocal range of the human voice. A typical bass has a range extending from around the E below the bottom of the bass clef to the E above middle C.

Note-A-Day Calendars

Sunday
August
16

2009

When rehearsing with a band, be sure to work with an organized set list. How do you want the tempo of your show to go?

Put together your ideal set list and be open to making changes to create the best overall flow for the show.

One of the first innovative choral composers of the Baroque was Claudio Monteverdi (1567-1643), a master of counterpoint.

Tuesday

May

19

2009

As you practice today, focus on your support. Is your rib cage staying lifted as you sing? If not, put both hands on either side of your rib cage as you sing to bring your awareness to any inward collapse.

Frank Sinatra once called rock and roll "the most brutal, ugly, degenerate, vicious form of expression it has been my displeasure to hear."

Saturday
August
15
2009

Record yourself singing a song. Listen to it and see if you can hear when your pitch is accurate or inaccurate. As you adjust any pitch, be sure to sing the correct vowel.

In the Middle Ages, sacred music was called plainsong. It consisted of a single unaccompanied melody with words in the Latin.

Wednesday

May

20

2009

Every time you perform, you gain more strength and confidence in your voice.

Seek out performance opportunities. Perform at least one song at a karaoke bar or retirement home, either solo or with accompaniment (using an instrument or recording).

Guitar sales escalated from 228,000 in 1950 to over 2.3 million in 1971.

Friday
August
14
2009

Review the "Three Areas" from the preface.

As you sing, experiment with moving between "traditional" musicality and "radical" musicality. Start with the extremes: completely traditional, then completely radical.

Slowly, begin moving between the two extremes, creating new blends of the two. You may arrive at choices you would like to use in performance.

Chamber music is played by small groups, such as a string quartet or piano trio.

Thursday

May

21

2009

As a gift to yourself, look at your wish list of music, instruments, and equipment. What is the most important item that would move you forward as a musician?

Tell someone about it, or start saving so you can buy it yourself!

A hymn is a simple religious song in several stanzas.

Thursday

August

13

2009

How do you promote yourself? Do you have business cards, flyers, or a website where people can find information about you and your performing?

Focus on the image you want to project, the energy you want others to receive, as you work on your promotional materials. Get professional support as needed.

"Music is love in search of a word." - Sidney Lanier

Note-A-Day Calendars

Friday

May

22

2009

If you go out tonight, notice how your voice is affected tomorrow by: what you have to drink or eat, being in an environment with smoke, or how much sleep you get.

If you like to drink, avoid beer the night before a performance. Drinking beer will make you sing flat the next day since it relaxes everything!

The earliest notated music of western Europe is Gregorian Chant, along with a few other types of chant that were later revealed by the Catholic church.

Wednesday

August

12

2009

If you need more information on vocal health or how different drugs can affect the voice, visit www.ncvs.org, the website for the National Center for Voice and Speech, or go to www.voicedoctor.com.

A cantata (Italian, sung) is a vocal composition that is accompanied by instruments and usually contains more than one movement.

Saturday
May
23
2009

Practice vocal exercises today that work on expanding your range. Practice vocal glides, five tone scales, eight tone scales, and arpeggios (see glossary). Begin in your lower register, and work to the highest part of your upper register.

"Whenever society gets too stifling and the rules get too complex, there's some sort of musical explosion" - Slash

Note-A-Day Calendars

Tuesday

August

11

2009

Practice singing the following intervals (an interval is the distance between two notes) in the keys of B and E:

augmented fourth (A4); 3 steps; Example: B to E#
diminished fifth (D5-also called tritone); 3 steps; Example: B to F

On your pitch pipe, play the higher note, then the lower note. Sing both. Memorize the sound.

"Music is a higher revelation than philosophy." - Ludwig van Beethoven

Note-A-Day Calendars

Sunday

May

24

2009

Sight-read a piece of music you've never seen or sung before from start to finish. Go as slow as you want, but do not correct mistakes or go back. When you get to the end, stop and put the music away.

If you can't read music, refer to the rhythms in the preface, find a simple piece of music, and see if you can clap the rhythm to it.

An example of a major sixth interval is heard in the first two notes of the television network NBC's theme, "N - B - C."

Note-A-Day Calendars

Monday

August

10

2009

Create the perfect practice space. Does it inspire you to sing? Is the space and the set-up comfortable? Are the colors inviting? What do you need to add or take away to make it feel right for you? Make it organized, easy to access, private, clean, and inspirational.

In the Romantic period, composers used music to highlight national identity.

Note-A-Day Calendars

Monday

May

25

2009

The tempo at which you practice your exercises is important.

Take one exercise and sing it at your regular tempo. Then sing it just a bit slower. Then again, a bit faster than normal. Notice the difference.

If needed, sing with a metronome (or CD/tape) to find a consistent practice tempo for each exercise you use.

"Dynamics" refers to the softness or loudness of a sound or note.

Note-A-Day Calendars

Sunday

August

9

2009

List of things to bring to a performance:

- Music and music stand
- Props
- Costumes
- Water or tea
- Business cards and promotional materials
- Throat drops with lemon
- Make-up and toiletries
- Directions, contact info, and maps

"Music is the universal language of mankind." - Henry Wadsworth Longfellow

Tuesday

May

26

2009

Put on a recording that you like. Improvise over it using any syllable you like, without singing any of the same parts that are on the recording. Do this for at least one song.

"In opera, there is always too much singing." - Claude Debussy

Saturday
August
8
2009

Singing requires our body to be strong, yet free. This takes great awareness.

Practice singing in front of a mirror. Pay attention to your posture. Notice if any particular part of your body tenses unnecessarily when you sing (such as your neck, shoulders, arms, hands, knees, etc). Stretch, then shake out any tension, and see if you can change your habit of "holding."

The "Hallelujah Chorus," from George Frederic Handel's "Messiah," is one of the most famous choruses of all time.

Note-A-Day Calendars

Wednesday

May

27

2009

Improvise the following "items," imagining your voice is: Jell-O, steel, glue, Velcro, silk, and water.

Come up with your own!

Pianissimo means "very soft."

Note-A-Day Calendars

Friday

August

7

2009

As you sing today, sing from your heart.

As you are singing, keep your awareness on your heart. See if you can feel it while you sing.

During their 30-odd year career, Black Sabbath have had 29 different members.

Note-A-Day Calendars

Thursday

May

28

2009

Research your favorite genre of vocal music on the Internet. What new music would you like to hear?

Write down any artists and titles that interest you and find them (at your local music store, library, or online).

Sempre means "always."

Note-A-Day Calendars

Thursday

August

6

2009

Arrive at any audition at least 15 minutes early. Give yourself extra time for travel and for becoming familiar with the audition space. Find a place where you can be by yourself to get grounded and focused.

"As any jazz musician knows, it takes flexibility and adaptability for improvisation to create beauty." - Doc Childre and Bruce Cryer

Friday

May

29

2009

Validate yourself today. Write 10 things that you enjoy about your voice.

Keep this list around where you can occasionally look at it.

Prince played 27 different instruments on his debut album "For You."

Wednesday

August

5

2009

Take a break from your regular practice routine today. Instead, just listen to some of your favorite singers.

For at least 10 minutes, only listen to what you hear in their voices that is new and inspiring to you.

Calando means "gradually softer and slower."

Saturday

May

30

2009

Find the music for a jazz standard and read it, following along as best you can (www.RealBook.us and www.8notes.com/scores have some to follow along with).

If you don't read music, find any simple sheet music and clap the rhythms (using the rhythmic guide in the preface).

A series is a fixed arrangement of pitches or rhythms throughout a composition (called a "serial composition").

Tuesday

August

4

2009

When you're first learning the style of a song, keep counting mentally, even during the rests. You will develop a more solid understanding of how the music is constructed, and you'll have an easier time singing in "the pocket."

"Singing has always seemed to me the most perfect means of expression. It is so spontaneous. And after singing, I think the violin. Since I cannot sing, I paint." - Georgia O'Keefe

Note-A-Day Calendars

Sunday

May

31

2009

As the holiday season begins, take really good care of yourself so you can stay healthy and sing joyfully.

Write down three things you will do during this season to stay balanced.

"Music is the wine that fills the cup of silence." - Robert Fripp

Note-A-Day Calendars

Monday

August

3

2009

Keep your audition songs fresh by continually striving for emotional vulnerability. Allow your gestures to arise from this real emotion, not a staged or rehearsed movement. If you're challenged by this, consider taking an acting class to learn more acting techniques.

Some interesting instruments of the Renaissance were lutes, shawms, krummhorns, and small version of trumpets and trombones.

Note-A-Day Calendars

Monday

June

1

2009

Choose a new song that you want to learn and start by listening to it over and over again. Go phrase by phrase, singing “la” for the melody, adding the words only if you feel ready.

Review your musical goals today.

Note-A-Day Calendars

Sunday
August
2
2009

Sing the following patterns in the keys of C# and F#:

1 3 2 4 3 4 2 1
1 2 1 4 2 1
3 1 2 3 4 2 1
5 3 4 2 1 7 1

Sing first using numbers, then using the names of the actual notes.

Opus means “work.” Opera is plural for opus.

Tuesday

June

2

2009

The vowels we know well are: a, e, i, o, u. Sometimes, y and w become vowels when singing.

Look at the lyrics of the song(s) you are working on and find any words that begin with y or w. Since they start with an oo, begin them before the beat, so the next vowel can come on the beat (i.e."where" becomes "oo" followed by "eh" on the beat).

4/4 time is classified as "simple quadruple," due to its four beats that can be divided into two notes.

Note-A-Day Calendars

Saturday

August

1

2009

Practice a song today, without singing. Read through the music, listen to a recording of it, or just visualize yourself singing it.

Review your musical goals today.

Wednesday
June
3
2009

Check out the following websites for further information on finding songs and lyrics:

www.aria-database.com
www.leoslyrics.com
www.musicnotes.com

"Music is the poetry of the air." - Richter

Friday

July

31

2009

Most people have relative pitch -- the ability to match a note they hear without necessarily knowing the name of the note. Very few people have perfect pitch -- the ability to sing a precise note without any outside source.

Practice sight-reading a piece of music today and don't expect yourself to do it perfectly. Sight-reading is a learned skill that takes time and repetition. The more you do it, the better your pitch recognition will become.

A libretto is the complete book of words for an opera, oratorio, or cantata.

Note-A-Day Calendars

Thursday

June

4

2009

Spend five minutes writing about why you love to sing. What calls to you through your voice? What does your heart long to express?

Writing can help clarify your deeper desires, and inspire you during the times when you feel down.

Recitative, a form of music used in operas, oratorios, cantatas, and similar styles, is melodic speech set to music, or a descriptive narrative song in which the music follows the words.

Thursday

July

30

2009

To help deal with nerves before auditions/performances, think of it as another opportunity to sing in a theatre or on a stage. Doing so can help it not feel so "loaded".

Remember that those listening want you to be "the one". They are supporting you completely.

Mozart's choral music generally does not represent his best work, with a few exceptions (such as the "Requiem mass in D minor").

Friday
June
5
2009

Lay or sit in a relaxed position and close your eyes.

Choose a song that you have memorized, and that is challenging for you to sing. Imagine yourself singing that song. As you imagine, pay attention to your body. Do you tense up or change your breathing at any point in the song?

If so, isolate that part of the song. See if you can relax any tense body parts and maintain deep, even breathing as you imagine singing that part. This may take numerous times before you can do it - take your time.

When you've got it, put on the accompaniment and sing the song.

There are 15 major and minor key signatures.

Note-A-Day Calendars

Wednesday

July

29

2009

One of the overall goals in studying technique is that eventually the technique becomes "automatic".

Sing a song, focusing on the details of your technique. Sing it again, this time expressing the music from your heart.

Work this way with every song you sing today, first the technique, then the artistry.

"Were it not for music, we might in these days say, the beautiful is dead."
- Benjamin Disraeli

Saturday

June

6

2009

Sing the following patterns in the keys of Bb and Eb:

1 3 2 4 3 4 2 1
1 2 1 4 2 1
3 1 2 3 4 2 1
5 3 4 2 1 7 1

Sing first using numbers, then using the names of the actual notes.

Iscathamiya is Zulu call-and-response, a cappella choral music sung by men from South Africa.

Tuesday
July
28
2009

Choose a new song that you have a recording of with solo voice and accompaniment. To strengthen your sight-reading skills, learn as much of the vocal part as you can in five minutes.

Focus on notes and rhythms, singing only a single vowel. Add words only after you've got the notes and rhythms.

"The Chipmunks," Alvin, Simon, and Theodore, were named after executives at Liberty Records by their creator, Ross Bagdasarian, who used the stage name David Seville.

Note-A-Day Calendars

Sunday

June

7

2009

Before you sing today, take a short walk around the block.

Notice the sky, the trees, and the air. Notice your breathing. Let your breathing be deep and even.

Enjoy this refreshed feeling as you begin your practice.

The "Star-Spangled Banner" became the US national anthem in 1931. Prior to that, it was "My Country 'Tis of Thee.""

Note-A-Day Calendars

Monday

July

27

2009

Looking at the Circle of Fifths in the preface, start with an F# minor scale and name every note.

Test your memory as much as possible. Go through the C# minor scale, making note of the ones you don't have memorized.

The rhythm of melody is often based on the inflections of language and the physical rhythms of dance.

Monday

June

8

2009

Improvise using attitudes or emotions, such as loving, frustrated, joyful, disgusted, etc. You can sing words, syllables, or just sounds to help express yourself.

Rap has roots in diverse styles, including West African griots (poets and praise-singers), spirituals, scat, blues, jump-rope rhymes, and doo-wop.

Note-A-Day Calendars

Sunday

July

26

2009

Think about the sound equipment that you use. Is there anything you would like that you don't have yet?

Make a list, prioritize it, and start a savings plan to insure that you will be able to purchase what you need.

Billboard's "Hot 100" chart debuted in 1958, with Ricky Nelson in the #1 slot with "Poor Little Fool."

Note-A-Day Calendars

Tuesday

June

9

2009

Improvise using a "drone": one constant pitch that you sing against.

Use any instrument to create the drone, or make a tape of yourself singing one pitch (a lower pitch will work better) continuously for five minutes. How does the drone effect your improvisation?

A coda is a closing section to a piece of music.

Note-A-Day Calendars

Saturday

July

25

2009

Sing the following patterns in the keys of G# and D#:

1 3 2 4 3 4 2 1
1 2 1 4 2 1
3 1 2 3 4 2 1
5 3 4 2 1 7 1

Sing first using numbers, then using the names of the actual notes.

Melba toast is named after Australian opera singer Dame Nellie Melba (1861-1931).

Note-A-Day Calendars

Wednesday

June

10

2009

Take a song you know well and sing it, ignoring how it's "supposed" to sound. Change the rhythms, pitches, dynamics, speed, etc., in any way you choose.

You can write out your changes, or just improvise your new version. Do this several times, but change it each time.

"A good composer is slowly discovered; a bad composer is slowly found out."
- Ernest Newman

Friday

July

24

2009

Choosing appropriate literature is important for many reasons. To develop your voice, you need to sing a combination of classical music (art song or operatic literature) to build your vocal strength and agility, along with other musical styles that you enjoy.

In the studio, work on music that you wouldn't necessarily perform, just so you can build your voice.

In the world, sing whatever style you prefer, and your voice will be stronger and more versatile.

To find appropriate literature for your voice type, consult an experienced voice teacher.

When Pink Floyd's "Dark Side Of The Moon" finally fell off of Billboard's Hot 200 Album list in October 1988, it had set a record of 741 weeks on the chart.

Thursday

June

11

2009

What does your performance resume look like? Possible categories to include are: Performance Experience (most recent to least recent, dates not needed), Education and Training, Choral Experience: Soloist, Solo Recitals, Recordings, Honors/Awards.

Take some time today to create/update your performance resume (if you have little or no experience, make one up that you'd like to have).

Originally, rapping was called Mc-ing and accompanied Dj-ing.

Note-A-Day Calendars

Thursday
July
23
2009

Listen to a professional recording of a song you are practicing, and focus on the singer's phrasing (a musical phrase extending from one breath to the next). How does their choice of phrasing and breathing allow them to express the emotions of the song?

Based in San Francisco, CA, Chanticleer is the only full-time classical vocal ensemble in the United States.

Note-A-Day Calendars

Friday

June

12

2009

At an audition, be sure to express dynamic variation in your songs, but don't get caught up in the "bigness" of your voice. You don't have to try to prove to anyone that you can sing. Just be fully committed and present to the experience. Your love of singing will shine through!

In the Romantic period, a "miniature" was a short, evocative composition for piano.

Note-A-Day Calendars

Wednesday

July

22

2009

Create some simple flash cards that list different gestures on each one, such as: one hand to heart, hands on hips, right hand forward, one hand in fist, etc.

Sing a song you know well. Pick up a new flash card every 10-15 seconds and do the gesture listed.

Continue to work with this, keeping the gestures you like, discarding the rest.

"Extraordinary how potent cheap music is." - Noel Coward

Note-A-Day Calendars

Saturday

June

13

2009

To begin songwriting, take a phrase and speak it with inflection. Which words did you emphasize?

Sing a simple melody with this phrase, putting emphasis on the emphasized words by using a pitch that is contrasting (higher or lower) or a note value that is a little longer. Does your new melody add to the meaning of the phrase or detract from it?

"Life can't be all bad when, for ten dollars, you can buy all the Beethoven sonatas and listen to them for ten years." - William F. Buckley, Jr.

Note-A-Day Calendars

Tuesday

July

21

2009

Review the "Three Areas" from the preface.

As you sing, experiment with moving between relaxation and tension in your body and face. Start with the extremes: complete relaxation, then complete tension.

Slowly, begin moving between the two extremes, creating new blends of the two. You may arrive at choices you would like to use in performance.

"I can't stand to sing the same song the same way two nights in succession."
– Billie Holiday

Note-A-Day Calendars

Sunday

June

14

2009

When learning a song in a new language, follow these steps:

- Listen to a recording of it
- Make a translation sheet: write down the text, then a word for word translation
- Speak the text
- Learn to appreciate the sound of the language
- Vocalize the melody, finding a sense of the line
- Put the text with the melody (slowly at first)
- Record yourself singing it and listen carefully to the nuances
- Memorize it

Harmonics are pure, individual sounds that are part of any musical tone.

Note-A-Day Calendars

Monday

July

20

2009

To increase the expressiveness of your face, spend a few minutes doing face exercises: stretch your face as wide as you can, then make it as tight as you can. Repeat a few times.

Pretend you are a cow, chewing in big, wide circles. Switch directions. Massage your jaw.

Create your own facial exercises as well.

"Country music is three chords and the truth." - Harlan Howard

Note-A-Day Calendars

Monday
June
15
2009

Find a four-part song (soprano, alto, tenor, and bass) and sight-read a part other than your own. Sopranos, sing the alto part; tenors sing the baritone or bass part, etc.

"Music is the greatest communication in the world. Even if people don't understand the language that you're singing in, they still know good music when they hear it." - Lou Rawls

Note-A-Day Calendars

Sunday

July

19

2009

Create a list of songs you're currently working on. Choose one song and memorize the first verse today.

The Vocal Majority, a men's chorus of over 150 singers from Dallas, TX, is billed as the premier pops chorus in America.

Note-A-Day Calendars

Tuesday

June

16

2009

If you are singing pop music, country, folk, or jazz, always use a microphone so that you don't push your voice too much.

Tchaikovsky was financed by a wealthy widow for 13 years, and, at her request, they never met.

Saturday
July
18
2009

Some performance tips:

• Choose music that you like to sing
• Choose a diverse range of songs; vary tempos, keys, moods, characters, etc.
• Practice anything you want to say about the pieces, allow time for applause, etc.
• Set aside plenty of time before performing to set up and relax
• Create a routine to help you relax immediately before singing, such as deep breathing, massage, meditation, visualization, etc.

The Baroque period coincided with the birth of opera.

Note-A-Day Calendars

Wednesday

June

17

2009

Journal for 5-10 minutes on why you sing, what it means to you, and how it affects you.

Some questions to guide you: Why do you enjoy singing? How does singing make your life better?

Feel free to come up with your own questions as well, either in place of or in addition to the above questions.

An exposition is the first section of a sonata that presents the main musical themes.

Note-A-Day Calendars

Friday
July
17
2009

Improvise using "soundscapes", sliding all around using mostly vowels, focusing on expressing your feelings without words of any kind.

Try this with accompaniment, then without.

"Secular music" is non-religious in nature.

Thursday

June

18

2009

Imagine that today is the last day that you'll ever sing again.

What would you choose to sing? How does imagining this affect your singing?

"I've always felt rock and roll was very, very wholesome music." - Aretha Franklin

Note-A-Day Calendars

Thursday

July

16

2009

Focus on your breathing as you sing today. Breathe as low as possible, feeling expansion happen all around your body, like an inner tube. As you try this, notice how your low belly expands, your ribs expand, and even your lower back moves outward.

As you sing, focus on keeping the lower belly moving inwards, while maintaining the rib cage in its expanded state.

Country singer Waylon Jennings was a guitar player in Buddy Holly's backup band. He gave up his plane seat to J.P. Richardson just moments before it took off. The plane crashed, killing all on board, including Buddy Holly.

Note-A-Day Calendars

Friday

June

19

2009

Your musical ear is your strongest guide in creating fulfilling music. Don't let any vocal technique or functional idea take the place of your musical ear.

Trust yourself. As your skills increase, your confidence will also increase.

Keep your vocal chords hydrated: drink eight glasses of water a day (preferably in the morning), and avoid caffeine and alcohol, which act as diuretics (substances that increase urination) and cause the body to lose water.

Note-A-Day Calendars

Wednesday

July

15

2009

Listen to a professional recording of a song you are practicing, and focus on the details of the style. Are the vowels darker (operatic), brighter (pop/country), or somewhere in between? Are the consonants crisp or emphasized less? Now sing the song, trying to match their style as much as possible.

Sing it again, within the style, but use your own interpretation.

"Singing becomes a form of therapy." - Placido Domingo

Note-A-Day Calendars

Saturday
June
20
2009

As you prepare any type of advertising materials (business cards, brochures, website etc.), it's good to have: testimonials about your singing, photos from different performances, and clear, concise information about yourself and your performing.

Set a time to gather and prepare these materials and information.

"We are always more anxious to be distinguished for a talent which we do not possess, than to be praised for the fifteen which we do possess." - Mark Twain

Tuesday

July

14

2009

Think of an animal. Improvise something that captures the personality of that animal. Some animals to try are cats, dogs, snakes, fish, mice, and birds.

"Use the talents you possess, for the woods would be very silent if no birds sang except the best." - Henry Van Dyke

Sunday

June

21

2009

When preparing for performance, remember that most people perform at 65% of what they rehearsed. So be gentle with yourself. Don't expect so much.

"You are the music while the music lasts." - T.S. Eliot

Note-A-Day Calendars

Monday
July
13
2009

Nodules or nodes are callouses that develop on the vocal folds from misuse or overuse. They can develop very quickly, but can be healed quickly as well. Some of the symptoms are hoarseness, vocal fatigue, and the inability to create a clean sound.

If you have any question about the health of your vocal folds, consult an ear, nose and throat specialist (ENT).

"If I were to begin life again, I would devote it to music. It is the only cheap and unpunished rapture upon earth." - Sydney Smith

Monday

June

22

2009

In honor of Valentine's Day, sing a dearly loved song as a gift to yourself for all the work that you do as a singer.

"There is nothing in the world so much like prayer as music is." - William P. Merrill

Sunday

July

12

2009

Look up and memorize the definitions for the following terms: rubato, sforzando, sostenuto, tutti, and voce.

The Animals' 1964 single "House Of The Rising Sun" was the first No.1 hit to have a playing time of more than four minutes.

Note-A-Day Calendars

Tuesday

June

23

2009

Five minutes a day of focused practice will yield better results than 15 minutes of unfocused practice. And, five minutes a day is more than not practicing at all.

Focus on the quality of your practice time, rather than the quantity. Five minutes a day adds up to over 30 hours a year!

There is one recorded case of the human voice being detected at a distance of 10.5 miles (17km), across still water at night.

Note-A-Day Calendars

Saturday

July

11

2009

Break down areas of practice into smaller categories.

Instead of just warming up, divide it into physical warm-ups, scales, arpeggios, etc. Instead of just learning a song, break it down into researching it, learning the melody, working on the rhythms, isolating difficult parts, memorizing it, etc.

Set smaller goals. They are easier to reach, less overwhelming, and provide more motivation to continue.

Overtone singing (or overtone chanting, harmonic singing, or harmonic chant) is where the singer manipulates the harmonic resonances (or formants) created as air travels from the lungs, past the vocal folds, and out the lips.

Wednesday

June

24

2009

Today, sing only music that speaks deeply to your heart. Imagine that your heart has no boundaries, only abundant freedom to fully express itself.

Reflect on what it's like to only sing music that moves you, rather than music that you're "supposed" to sing.

During the early nineteenth century, opera composers su
Weber used German folk stories for the themes

Friday
July
10
2009

At the beginning of vocal training, power (volume) and intensity are one and the same. As you progress, you'll be able to separate them, singing softly (piano) with the same intensity that you sing loudly (forte).

Sing with dynamic variation today. Always maintain a balanced voice, not overblown or wimpy, but clear and ringing.

Music composed with natural sounds and recorded electronically is called "musique concrete."

Note-A-Day Calendars

Thursday
June
25
2009

Review the "Three Areas" from the preface.

As you sing a song you know well, experiment with moving between singing and speaking. Start with the extremes: completely sung, then completely spoken.

Slowly, begin moving between the two extremes, creating new blends of the two. You may arrive at choices you would like to use in performance.

In the Baroque period, composers became aware of music from countries and regions other than their own.

Note-A-Day Calendars

Thursday

July

9

2009

Review the “Three Areas” from the preface. Choose a piece you have memorized.

Working with characterization, experiment with the opposites of “who you are and how you perceive yourself” and “your role or who you want to become”.

Sing it first as one, then as the other. Then begin moving slowly between them, creating new blends of the two personae as you do. You may arrive at choices you would like to use in performance.

The earliest operatic masterpieces were composed in Florence, Italy by Claudio Monteverdi.

Friday

June

26

2009

What is the most frustrating aspect of your singing right now? When you experience this during your practice, what do you do?

Instead of trying to change this problem (yet one more time), embrace it! Simply shift your attitude about it, and do nothing else.

Dr. Joel Funk, professor of psychology at Plymouth State College in New Hampshire, found that 50% of people who have near-death experiences hear music, which they describe as "music with a beautiful, floating sound."

Note-A-Day Calendars

Wednesday

July

8

2009

Sing a challenging phrase and notice if your articulation is clear.

If not, speak (rather than sing) the phrase in rhythm, noticing the syllabic stress of the language.

Sing it again. If you're rhythmically accurate, your articulation will be clearer.

"The only thing better than singing is more singing." - Ella Fitzgerald

Saturday

June

27

2009

A fun way to remember good singing posture is to imagine that you are a puppet with a string attached to the top of your head. Someone pulls the string, gently elongating your spine upwards and lifting your rib cage.

Now you're ready to breathe low and sing fully!

Cold air and water cause the tissue of the larynx to contract, making it harder to produce a full, clear tone.

Note-A-Day Calendars

Tuesday
July
7

2009

Recording in a studio is a very different experience from recording with a live audience. The studio offers a polished sound, while the live audience offers an energized experience. What is one way you can bring the inspiration of the audience into the studio?

The average adult male's vocal chords vibrate 120 times per second, while the average adult female's vibration is 220 times per second, creating a higher pitch.

Note-A-Day Calendars

Sunday

June

28

2009

Singers are often challenged by sinus issues. Remember that the drainage from the sinuses does not touch the vocal folds. It goes down the back of the throat and into the esophagus.

The piriform sinuses (located just above the larynx) are the only sinuses that lubricate the larynx. There is no way to flush the piriform sinuses. If you have sinus issues, consider seeing a medical professional.

Singers tend to raise the chin when reaching for the high notes, but this actually constricts the airway, making it harder to hit the notes.

Monday
July
6
2009

It's never too late to begin again! If you are starting vocal training and are over the age of 60, it will take more time to build your vocal strength than if you are 20. As we age, elastin fibers decrease and collagin fibers increase in our muscles, causing our vocal folds to get more rigid.

After breath control, diction is the most important aspect of singing.

Note-A-Day Calendars

Monday

June

29

2009

Perform in front of a mirror. How do you look? Relaxed? Excited? Uncomfortable?

Change your expressions and/or gestures and notice how much more freedom you can access in your body and voice.

The term "riff," a short, catchy musical idea, entered musical slang in the 1920s. It is used primarily in discussing forms of rock music or jazz.

Sunday

July

5

2009

Sing a C major scale using the syllables do (1), re (2), mi (3), fa (4), sol (5), la (6), ti (7), do (8), with each syllable corresponding to the note in the scale.

With your pitch pipe, play the root (first) note, then the second note. Sing both, using syllables do and re.

Play the root note, then the third note; sing both using do and mi.

Play the root note and the fourth note; sing both using do and fa.

Continue doing this for the whole scale, ascending and descending.

In Iceland, the traditional song style known as tvísöngur ("twin-singing") goes back to the Middle Ages, and is still taught in schools today. In this style, a melody is sung against itself, typically in parallel fifths.

Tuesday

June

30

2009

Once you've done some vocal exercises, see what kinds of "ugly" or "weird" sounds you can sing today!

Experiment with contrasts: really low or high, fast or slow, sharp or flat, sliding or staccato, gibberish or words, wobbly or straight tone, raspy or clear, etc. Enjoy the freedom to create all types of sounds with your voice.

Broadly speaking, plainsong (also known as plainchant) is the name given to the body of traditional songs used in the liturgies of the Roman Catholic Church.

Saturday

July

4

2009

Notice your thoughts as you practice today. Are you thinking ahead to what you're going to sing, or dwelling on what you previously sang?

See if you can let any distracting thoughts pass through your mind and return your attention to what you're presently singing.

In quintina singing, a quartet sits in an inward-facing circle in four-part harmony, manipulating their vowels and timbre to create a virtual fifth voice produced from the harmonics.

Wednesday

July

1

2009

Listen to a recording of yourself singing anything. As you listen, notice if you are truly listening (as if you've never heard yourself before) or if you are listening with a preconceived idea of how it should or should not sound.

Review your musical goals today.

Friday

July

3

2009

Do some improvisation using children's songs. Use silly voices, sing with contrasts (loud or soft, fast or slow), and make-up new verses. If possible, sing some of them with kids.

Lower register notes require more air output.

Thursday

July

2

2009

Good singing takes strength and stamina.

When you're in good vocal shape, your voice shouldn't get tired, but your body might. Do some exercises to strengthen your torso and upper chest, such as sit-ups, push-ups, or lifting weights.

"It is so important that you use simplicity in your playing and in your music."
– James Burton, lead guitarist for Elvis Presley, Ricky Nelson, Emmylou Harris, John Denver, Gram Parsons, etc.